Let Me
Introduce You To
My Father

A Study on the Nature of God

Dale E. Phillips

DRYDEN PUBLISHERS

CONTENTS

INTRODUCTION

How can I thrive, or even survive, in this fast-paced computerized society? Some say you must look inward and discover "who I am". Others suggest you must look outward at the needs of those around you. Both are needed but neither will be deeply fulfilling until you have looked upward and discovered "why I am". You were created to glorify God (Isaiah 43:7,21), and in the process of glorifying Him, you will lift your life to the place of glory God intended.

The most insulting response you can make to God is apathy. To acknowledge that God exists and claim some allegiance to Him, but to do so with carelessness and indifference is the ultimate put-down. How could you live before the awesome Creator and Sustainer of the universe and offer only stiff and minimal compliance? I believe God would actually prefer for us to yell at Him as yawn at Him.

WARFARE ON APATHY

I hereby proclaim open warfare on apathy. The following lessons will attempt to attack apathy at its root cause: a failure to know and understand God. Apathy pervades the non-Christian bulk of our society. Why are people so difficult to interest in spiritual matters? First, they are tragically caught up in a doomed pursuit of happiness. Many people have experienced painful failures trying to find fulfillment and security in material possessions and physical pleasures. They are periodically depressed and at times become bogged down in often incredible escapist activities. Spiritual concepts and words do not easily penetrate such troubled minds. Also, many are understandably disillusioned and turned off by organized religion. Financial and sexual scandals have rocked professed Bible-believing, spirit-filled, born-again leaders and groups. Where are people to turn for answers to their deep spiritual yearnings?

APATHY AND OUR VIEW OF THE FATHER

And what of the church? Apathy has also spread its life-numbing cloud over multitudes of church members. Many, hounded by guilt, still go to church and walk through the motions. They do their duty, but they never experience nor exhibit to others the exciting and

1

joyful relationship God intended for His children to have as they live in Christ and as His Spirit lives in them.

It all begins with a wrong view of the heavenly Father. We have been deluded into thinking this is what He wants, but our Father is most expressive about what He likes, and about what even delights Him! It is time for us to look at His words and listen and respond to Him.

We sometimes treat the Bible like a long, complex story from which we are to struggle to extract just the right laws, commands and rules which will please God. But why is the Bible such a thick volume? Hammurabi, an ancient Babylonian king, chiselled his entire code of life on one eight-foot tall stone pillar. And God etched His basic laws to Israel on two tablets of stone which Moses could lug up and down a craggy mountainside.

WHAT'S THE BIBLE ALL ABOUT?

The Bible was written primarily to reveal the nature of God. It is brimming with interactions between God and people, and in this real-life drama we discover the true identity and exciting Person of God. He is convinced that when we know and understand Him, we will not be able to withhold our praise. It will jump to our lips and control our lives. To know Him is to love Him! Hear His own words as He tells you what He wants above all else for you.

Jeremiah 9:23-24:

> *This is what the Lord says: "Let not the wise man boast of his wisdom or the strong man boast of his strength or the rich man boast of his riches, but let him who boasts boast about this: that he understands and knows Me, that I am the Lord who exercises kindness, justice and righteousness on earth, for in these I delight," declares the Lord.*

These lessons are presented to help you confront the God of the universe. You may be pleasantly surprised at what you find, or even astounded, but you will never be bored. Thank you for allowing me to share this adventure. Let me introduce you to my Father.

Imagine yourself hiding in Eden's garden among some plush bushes watching as God completes the creation. You are the first to see the water teem with life.[1] A sixty-foot whale rolls to the surface and slaps his huge tail on the surf. "Awesome!" you gasp. The next day the landscape erupts with numberless wild animals.[2] An elephant nibbles at the bush beside you and your heart nearly stops.

Then God speaks, "Let us make man in our image, in our likeness."[3] Later He states simply, "it is not good for the man to be alone"[4] and there before you stand the first humans. Now suppose at this point God looked straight at you and said, "You, hiding in the bushes, do you have any questions?" What would you ask?

If I ever got my breath back, I believe I would ask God (in a reverent and shaking voice) "Father, why have you made these humans? What is it You want from them?"

Fortunately, God caused the Bible to be recorded and gave very high priority to answering such questions. Come explore this unique book with me as we seek to discover what God really wants with us. In this initial lesson we will consider three overriding desires God has expressed for our lives.

FIRST: HE WANTS US TO KNOW AND UNDERSTAND HIM

The message of Jeremiah 9:23-24 is emphatic.

> *This is what the Lord says, "Let not the wise man boast of his wisdom or the strong man boast of his strength or the rich man boast of his riches, but let*

---

[1]Genesis   1:20-23
[2]Genesis   1:24-25
[3]Genesis   1:26-27
[4]Genesis   2:18

him who boasts boast about this: that he understands
and knows Me, that I am the Lord, who exercises
kindness, justice, and righteousness on earth, for in
these I delight, " declares the Lord. "

Above all else our Father wants us to know and understand Him. He wants this to be the passionate center of our lives. He expects us to acknowledge Him as Lord but He also desires us to know in depth what kind of Father He is. Three qualities are specified here: kindness, justice and righteousness.

But can we really know and understand God? Read Romans 11:33-36. This seems to say the answer is no. His wisdom and judgments are not to be compared with our feeble efforts.[5] We must agree with Zophar the Naamathite that God's mysteries and limits are higher than the heavens, longer than the earth and wider than the sea,[6] while ours have more the dimensions of a mud puddle. Yet despite all this, God has said He really delights in our knowing and understanding Him. Mission impossible? We all have people who are close to us who we know and understand. We don't know everything about them by any means; but what we do know, we appreciate and this is the basis for a growing relationship. Like a giant iceberg, we come to know and understand God first on the surface. Then deeper and deeper we go... and always there is more, so much more.

Even without the Bible, the material universe we see around us reveals that there must be a God who possesses power far greater and more enduring than ours, and also a nature which is more than human.[7] But we need to understand much more about God than this to live successfully on this earth.

Moses was a man with a big problem. He was trying to lead perhaps two to three million reluctant people[8] through a wilderness to a place they had never seen. He was overwhelmed by the task.

---

[5]Isaiah 55:8-9;   Isaiah   40:12-15,18,25-26
[6]Job   11:7-9
[7]Romans 1:20; Psalm 19:1-6
[8]Exodus 12:37

4

God had appeared to him in the burning bush,[9] had shown His might at the Red Sea,[10] had given him the Law on the mountain[11] and was providing food for this mass of people.[12] But Moses needed more. He pleaded with God to "teach me your ways so that I may know You and continue to find favor with You."[13] He knew much about God but needed to experience God's nature personally. God's response was not another dazzling miracle or another list of laws but rather He vividly explained His nature to Moses.[14] This is what we need above all else; and praise be to God, He wants us to really know and understand His wondrous nature.

ALSO: HE WANTS US TO LOVE, OBEY AND PRAISE HIM

God wanted His people, Israel, to enjoy long fruitful lives.[15] In order for this to happen, He told them they must obey His commandments.[16] The most basic and most important commandment of all has always been to love God with all that is in us.[17] Jesus taught that by obeying God's commandments we remain in His love.[18]

Why are love and obedience inseparably tied to each other? Because above all else God desires a relationship with us. The very essence of His nature is love. We cannot know and please God unless we are filled to overflowing with this great truth: God is love.[19] All the obedience and sacrifice in the world is useless to God unless it is stirred by the love we have because we have to come to know and understand Him.[20]

---

[9] Exodus 3:1-6 (see also Acts 7:30)
[10] Exodus 14:15-31
[11] Exodus 20; 34
[12] Exodus 16:11-36; John 6:31
[13] Exodus 33:13
[14] Exodus 34:5-8
[15] Deuteronomy 4:40; 5:16
[16] Deuteronomy 6:1-3
[17] Deuteronomy 6:3-9; Matthew 22:36-40
[18] John 15:9-10
[19] I John 4:7-8

Jesus made an astounding statement: "If you love Me, you will obey what I command."[21] God declares that when we really know And understand who He is and what He is doing for us, we will obey Him! So irresistible is the nature of our Father that to really know Him is to love Him; and to love Him leaves no alternative but to live obediently in His nourishing, warming and compelling love. Our problem is that we have failed to look deeply at our Father and to be conquered by His goodness.

The reason we sin is because we miss the real purpose for our lives (sin literally means to miss the mark). In our desperation, we waste our lives in the frustrating pursuit of what can only be found in relationship with God. Read Deuteronomy 10:12-22. How beautifully this sums up the basic needs of our lives and God's way to fulfill these. We are to walk in love with God and do His commands which are for our good. He is a powerful God above allother powers. He is above human pettiness and freely provides for all, especially the weak and resourceless. We are to experience His great love and see the vastness of His tender mercy and break forth in praise of His wonderful nature.[22] This is what He wants from us. He has an ultimate desire. Let's look now at this.

FINALLY:

HE WANTS TO BE YOUR FATHER AND DWELL WITH YOU

Allow me to become more personal at this point. God has a great plan for all humanity,[23] but so special and personal is your Father that this plan has been suited to *your* needs. What is it God wants with you? Perhaps this will surprise you, but above all else, God desires to hear you say from the depths of your being and in an understanding way, "You are my Father and I am Your child." Can you believe this? The great God of the universe who made everything and owns everything... all He really wants is to hear you say, "I love you with all my heart, Father."

---

[20] I Corinthians 13:1-3
[21] John 14:15
[22] Ephesians 1:6,12,14
[23] Ephesians 3:10-11

With His great heart breaking because His people had turned from Him, He gently pleaded, "I thought you would call me 'Father' and not turn away from following Me."[24] "I have loved you with an everlasting love; I have drawn you with loving-kindness," He cried.[25]

Read carefully II Corinthians 6:14-7:1. Doesn't it start to come home to you? God hates idols or anything else that wedges itself between you and your relationship with Him. He wants to live with you and walk with you and "be a Father to you". And because He has promises... because he offers this security to you... because He has elevated you to such a lofty place from which no one can pull you down[26].... because He is eternally committed to your well-being[27] and will never forsake you,[28] because of all this, you are empowered to keep yourself pure and enjoy life abundant as He intended.[29]

If all this seems overwhelming and defies belief, I challenge you to continue this search with me. If you ever develop a clear vision of your God in all His glory, and allow Him an intimate place in your life, you will never again be apathetic and half-hearted in your walk with Him.

---

[24] Jeremiah 3:19
[25] Jeremiah 31:3
[26] John 10:28
[27] Jeremiah 29:11-12
[28] Hebrews 13:5-6
[29] John 10:10

1. According to Jeremiah 9:23-24, what should be our top priority? Why?

2. Must we know everything about God before we can begin to walk with Him? Discuss this.

3. What did Moses mean in Exodus 33:13 when he said "teach me Your ways so I may know You"?

4. What did God want Moses to know and understand about Him (Exodus 34:5-8)?

5. What commandment does God especially want impressed upon our children?

6. How are loving God and obeying God inter-related?

7. What connection is there in all this to "praising God"?

8. Describe the relationship God desires to have with you.

9. What will it take to achieve this kind of relationship?

2   FIRST ENCOUNTERS WITH THE FATHER

Our first lesson was an attempt to present an overview of God, but His boundless nature defies being fully captured on any film or artist's canvas or even the human mind. Yet to gaze on His beauty[1] and meditate on His character[2] are the most ennobling things we can do. Now we must dare to move closer and examine some of the intricate details of His glorious character.

This is the way I discovered the Taj Mahal in India. When I saw its famous white dome and its four lofty towers outlined from afar, I was struck with its great beauty. But moving closer proved even more intriguing. It seemed to loom larger and larger. Could it really be this massive? As I walked its rooms and porches, and examined its magnificent carved inlaid stones, I gained a deep admiration for the craftsmen who constructed this ancient wonder of the world. Later as I again turned to view its memorable outline, I had much more to think about and wonder at.

So it is with God, but so much more so. We struggle to grasp the vast overall greatness of Him, to gaze on His total beauty, but we need to constantly move closer and ponder distinctive features and marvelous details of His awesome nature. It is more than we can absorb in a lifetime; but each time we stand upon His holy ground[3] and enjoy His majestic presence[4] we will come closer to seeing Him in all His glory. In the process we will find ourselves being changed into His likeness.[5] The following lessons will offer glimpses into His intricate nature. We begin with the first encounters between God and the people He created.

---

[1] Psalm 27:4
[2] Psalm 1:2; 63:6; 77:12; 104:34; 119:148; 143:5-6
[3] Genesis 28:16-17; Exodus 3:5; Joshua 5:15; Acts 7:33
[4] Psalm 16:11; II Corinthians 3:16-18; II Peter 1:16-18
[5] II Corinthians 3:18; Romans 8:29; Colossians 3:10

When God is given opportunity to work openly in a situation, the result is always creative. By nature His voice, His breath, His touch, move things from formlessness and emptiness to orderly beauty and abundant fullness.

His first actions related to us were "in the beginning God created the heavens and the earth."[6] He speaks and darkness is dispelled by light,[7] the formless earth is crafted into an array of oceans, lakes, rivers, mountains, valleys and plains.[8] The empty globe responds to His voice and teems with plant life,[9] fish and fowl,[10] and millions of roaming animals.[11] And don't forget the sun, moon and stars[12] which have always been our perfect timekeepers and stand as visible witnesses to the unfathomable greatness of our Creator Father.[13] We cannot begin to count the stars but He knows each by name![14]

But not only is His voice creative;[15] His touch is life-inducing as well. "Let us make man in our image, in our likeness" He proclaimed,[16] and with His own hands He took inanimate dust... fashioning, imagining, shaping and sculpting, until His ultimate creation was complete. It looked like a clay man on the outside but had a God-shaped image deep within it's spirit. Then the creative

---

[6]Genesis 1:1
[7]Genesis 1:3-4
[8]Genesis 1:9-10
[9]Genesis 1:11-12
[10]Genesis 1:20-22
[11]Genesis 1:24-25
[12]Genesis 1:14-18
[13]Psalm 19:1-4
[14]Isaiah 40:25-26
[15]Psalm 33:6-9; 148:5
[16]Genesis 1:26-27; 5:1

breath of God breathed His life into the first man.[17], and every person since then is in reality a creative work of God.[18]

While we cannot fully comprehend the great "why questions" of creation, we can see that we are a part of the great eternal design of God. No accidents are we. No mere afterthought. And we are not forgotten toys. We were made in the very image of God. He made us with deliberate purpose and He has great plans for our lives.[19] We are the apple of His eye[20] and we, called by His name, are to bring glory to His name.[21] And He plans to bring you and me to glory as well.[22]

Then He touched man again. The living man. He removed one rib from him and crowned His creative work by making the first woman.[23] The fruitful and abundant earth was not enough. Even ruling over and caring for it was not enough.[24] It was all for him but it was not enough.[25] Having a splendid garden to live in and care for was not enough.[26] Adam named all the animals[27] but he was not one with them. Adam was more; Adam needed more. Always God wants to create and give more. "It is not good for the man to be alone. I will make a helper suitable for him."[28] And so He did. When Adam awoke, God had brought her to be with

---

[17]Genesis 2:7
[18]Psalm 102:18; 104:30; Isaiah 42:5
[19]Psalm 139:13-16; Jeremiah 29:11-12
[20]Psalm 17:8; Deuteronomy 32:10; Zechariah 2:8
[21]Isaiah 43:7,21
[22]Romans 8:30; Hebrews 2:10; Philippians 3:21; I Corinthians 15:35-58
[23]Genesis 2:21-22
[24]Genesis 1:26-28
[25]Genesis 1:29
[26]Genesis 2:8-15
[27]Genesis 2:20
[28]Genesis 2:18

him,.and when Adam saw her, he said something like "wow!"[29] Or as the Living Bible reads: "This is it!"

Humanity is dependent upon the Creator Father... dependent in all aspects. He gave us life and He sustains our lives,[30] and we must love Him, and serve Him, and obey Him, if we would be complete and whole.[31] God not only gave the man and woman their breath, their bread, their home and each other, He gave them law so they might not forget their dependence on Him. "You are free to eat from every tree in the garden; but you must not eat from the tree of the knowledge of good and evil, for when you eat of it you will surely die."[32]

Now He had given them everything. They enjoyed a satisfying oneness[33] in the delightful garden.and there was no guilt to cast gloom over their joy.[34] No looking over their shoulders, no embarrassment, no regret. No wonder we have called Eden the "Garden of Paradise".

THE FATHERS VIEW OF SIN

Satan and evil are real and potent forces in our world.[35] A brief scan of human history or the morning newspaper confirms this sad reality: our world is permeated with sin and evil. We could ponder deep questions like "Where did evil come from?" or "Who created Satan?" These questions will remain unanswered, but the fact will persist: Evil is a brutal force which exists. It was already present when humanity was created. We cannot understand it. We cannot defeat it with our strength. God did not intend for us to have to constantly struggle "against the powers of this dark world and

---

[29]Genesis 2:23 - According to Hebrew scholars, there is a sense of wonderment and excitement not captured in the usual English translations.
[30]Acts 17:35
[31]Ecclesiastes 12:13
[32]Genesis 2:16-17
[33]Genesis 2:24
[34]Genesis 2:25
[35]Job 1:7; Ephesians 2:2; I Peter 5:8; I John 5:19

12

against the spiritual forces of evil in the heavenly realms".[36] He planned for mankind to dwell in warm daily fellowship with Him in the garden. He planned to come to them in the cool of the day to celebrate together their relationship.[37]

But another voice was heard and heeded. Satan came to the woman.[38] Her sensitivity possibly made her more vulnerable to his wiles. So Satan suggests that God has withheld something of high value from His creation. "You will not surely die, for God knows that when you eat of it your eyes will be opened, and you will be like God, knowing good and evil."[39] It looked so good; and imagine, we could be like God. To be like God. She couldn't resist. And her husband, perhaps in his desire to remain one with her, could not resist his wife's urgings.[40] The woman had been deceived and had neglected to seek her husband's counsel. So much for oneness. The man had disobeyed the direct command given him by God Himself. Both actions were equally fatal.

Open joyful relationship with God died that day. God comes, as usual, and calls to them. But His voice does not bring them scampering to His side but rather slinking off quickly into the bushes.[41] "Where are you?" God calls. The man answers, "I heard you in the garden, and I was afraid because I was naked; so I hid."[42] Fear was born that day.

Painless existence died that day. Now they must leave the garden and vie for food with the thorns and thistles.[43] Childbirth would be a painful experience. And the relationship of man and woman would have a power-struggle aspect from now on.[44] In short, life

---

[36] Ephesians 6:12
[37] Genesis 3:8
[38] Genesis 3:1; I Timothy 2:14
[39] Genesis 3:4-5
[40] Genesis 3:6-7
[41] Genesis 3:8
[42] Genesis 3:9-10
[43] Genesis 3:17-19
[44] Genesis 3:16

would be a struggle. And they began to die physically. Cut off from the tree of life, they began to experience aging and to face life on a timetable which eventually must run out.[45] Listening to Satan was extremely costly. It always is.

"You will not surely die," Satan lied. He lies by nature,[46] and it is deadly to believe his lies. But God is a creator, not a destroyer. He always tells us the truth. His word is the essence of truth.[47] God cannot lie for it is contrary to His whole nature.[48]

Satan lied again. "You will be like God." He implied God was holding out on them, keeping them from something significant. But what is it God desired all along? Why were they there in the Garden? Why did He come each day? Was it not to be with them? Was it not so they could, by fellowshipping with Him, grow to be like Him?

Despite their arrogance and disobedience, He did not give up on mankind. He drives them from the garden but He makes them clothes of skins to replace the hasty fig leaf suits of their design.[49] He still loves them. He gives them children and tries to intervene in their children's struggles to keep them from evil.[50] He had not left humanity alone. He never has; He never will.

A MOMENT OF MUSING

Genesis chapter five relates the long lives of the descendants of Adam and Eve. They lived from 777 to 969 years each... except for Enoch.[51] For 65 years he seemed to struggle on his own. Then Methuselah was born. Now he began to walk with God. For 300 years he walked with God. He didn't die. One day God simply took him away with Him.

---

[45]Genesis 3:22-24
[46]John 8:44
[47]John 17:17
[48]Numbers 23:19; Titus 1:2; Hebrews 6:18
[49]Genesis 3:7, 21
[50]Genesis 4:1-26
[51]Genesis 5:21-24

T. Gnananandam, an elderly preacher in India, relates this possible interpretation. God and Enoch met often to walk and talk together. Each day they walked a little farther as the relationship grew closer. One day God said to Enoch, "Look, we have walked so far together, it is closer to My house than to go back to yours. Why don't you just come on home and live with Me." Enoch agreed and was never heard from on earth again. It was like Eden revisited.

God has not left us helpless and hopeless in this wicked world. He is forever the Creator. He is expert at making something beautiful and useful out of that which is dark, empty, formless... even that which is corrupt and sinful. His nature keeps coming through. Turn from the power of Satan to the power of God[52] and He will begin doing wondrous things with you. Creative things. Exciting things. He longs to make you a totally new creation.[53]

But this is not all of His nature. Just a very promising beginning. In the lessons before us we will keep uncovering more and more treasures. Deep treasures. Deep mysteries.[54] Let's keep exploring together.

---

[52]Acts 26:18

[53]II Corinthians 5:17; Galatians 6:15; Ephesians 2:10

[54]Colossians 1:27; 2:3

15

1. Contrast God and Satan. God is by nature _____. Satan is by nature_____.

2. Is God's creation limited to the six days of Genesis 1? What is included in His creative work?

3. Can you describe wrong ways to try to become like God and right ways to become like God?

4. Noting Genesis chapters 3 and 4, what observations can you make about how God views sin?

5. Are you your brother's keeper?

6. What seems to have transpired in the God/Enoch episode?

7. What seems to be the overriding purpose for which we were created?

8. How does the way God feels about you affect the way you approach life?

3   THE FATHER AND THE FATEFUL FLOOD

Seven-year-old daughters are delightful! .And unpredictable. One moment, when I have fixed her bicycle or taken her to lunch, I am the best dad in the world. But an hour later my words of correction can earn me the epitaph "the most terriblest dad in the whole world".

How desirous we all are to be the beloved and the best father. But our grave responsibilities demand that we deal firmly, even severely with behavior which can threaten the well-being of our children. And so it is with God: "The earth is the Lord's, and everything in it, the world, and all who live in it."[1]   God takes this responsibility most seriously... and most lovingly.

"Consider, therefore, the kindness and sternness of God."[2] As we examine these characteristics of God, let's look at them not as separate characteristics, but as part of the integral nature of our Father, for the God of the creation is also the God of the flood.

OUR "OMNI" GOD

Our view of the world is usually limited to the nightly news or the daily newspaper. Most of the time we are so busy with our own pursuits, we focus on only a minute portion of humanity, while one-third of the time we forget it all in blissful slumber.

But our God is not like us. His eyes are everywhere, taking in all that transpires.[3] Every baby born in every obscure thatch hut captures His attention. Every hurt, every cruelty and every act of kindness is taken in: "Nothing in all creation is hidden from God's sight."[4], and He never nods off to sleep.[5]

---

[1] Psalm 24:1
[2] Romans 11:22
[3] Proverbs 15:3
[4] Hebrews 4:13
[5] Psalm 121:4

God is not impressed with our computers and their capacity to store and then recall bits of data. From the dawn of creation until this very second, all has been eternally comprehended. Yet this enormous weight of facts has not distracted God from focusing in on even the smallest details of each individual life. Behold Psalm 139!

How concerned is God with you? How well does He know you? He knows every time you get up or down. He sees all you do and hears every word you speak and knows your every thought. There is no place you can go where the all-pervasive Spirit of God will not be there. No hole is dark enough, nor any situation terrible enough, to escape the caring presence of God. Sunlight, moonlight, no light... all are the same to His eyes. His hand is always there offering to help, to lift, to protect or perhaps to discipline if that's what is needed.

And when did the holy vigil begin? Long before you were born when He carefully knitted your very being together in your mother's womb. He saw you unformed, partly formed and then finally uniform and complete. He knows your every line, freckle and wrinkle, and He loves all of you, as you are. And He has a book on you... a book of hopes, dreams and promises. A book of designs, designs for a rich and useful life.

Without fail "the eyes of the Lord range throughout the earth to strengthen those whose hearts are fully committed to Him".[6] He longs to see the good in us and to enhance and build on it, but so many have turned their hearts from Him to serve themselves. They fall into the same trap as Eve and Adam, and it is a fatal trap.

During one period in history, virtually all people had fallen into this trap. They listened to the call of the Evil One. The wickedness of mankind became all-inclusive. Everyone was involved in hurtful and destructive behavior day and night. Their minds were totally polluted.[7] It was hopeless. There was no turning back to God now. God looked and He saw nothing good... except for one little man

---

[6] II Chronicles 16:9

[7] Genesis 6:5

and his family. He saw Noah because He was looking for Noah. Noah had rejected the self-centered plunge into destruction taken by his neighbors. He had guided his family to trust in God, and Noah found favor in the eyes of the Lord.[8]

GOD'S VIEW OF REBELLIOUS HUMANITY

God had had enough. Enough rebellion and cruelty. He could not put up with this forever,[9] yet He did not act in anger and haste. He waited patiently for one hundred and twenty more years.[10] He gave them time to repent, time for Noah to proclaim the need to return to what was right.[11] But they were beyond listening. Instead they scoffed: "Everything keeps going on the same since creation began."[12] "A flood, oh really?" they mused.

Through it all, God grieved.[13] Grieved that they were so hell-bent, so determined to shake their feeble fists in the face of God. He would deal with this situation. Thoroughly. With one sweeping washing He would start again fresh and clean.[14] He would give mankind a great second chance, and He hoped humanity would learn. You do not turn your back on God, for there is nowhere to turn... except to devastation and death. God may be kind and forgiving but He is not weak. He knows how to deal with the rebellious and the sinful. Ask the angels who sinned.[15] Try to find Sodom and Gomorrah.[16] Or consider Nadab and Abihu;[17] Korah, Dathan and Abiram;[18] Queen Jezebel;[19] Ananias and Sapphira;[20]

---

[8]Genesis 6:8-10

[9]Genesis 6:3

[10]Genesis 6:3; I Peter 3:19-20

[11]II Peter 2:5

[12]II Peter 3:3-4

[13]Genesis 6:6-9

[14]Genesis 6:7; 11-13

[15]II Peter 2:4

[16]II Peter 2:6; Genesis 19:24-25;Luke 17:28-29

[17]Leviticus 10:1-2

[18]Numbers 16:1-33

[19]I Kings 21:23; II Kings 9:10, 30-37

King Herod Agrippa I.[21] Indeed "it is a dreadful thing to fall into the hands of the living God".[22]

It is popular to doubt the flood account of Genesis 6-8, but why is this so? Is it because the earth does not bear the signs of such a universal upheaval and flood? Not at all. The signs of such a deluge are manifold and irrefutable. Quick-frozen mammoths in Siberia and seashells on mountain tops demand a catastrophic event like the flood. So why doubt the flood? For the same reason all miracles are suspect. They present a God with a mandate and people don't like mandates. A kindly old man God would be alright. A sugar daddy God would be great. But a God "who is over all and through all and in all"[23] is a bit much. Too intrusive, too demanding, and some foolishly think, too confining. Like people in Noah's day, they want to go on living without regard for God,[24] but such disdain is immediately demeaning and ultimately fatal to humanity. If we think we are resourceless in dealing with Satan's power and antics, this will be nothing compared with dealing with the wrath of a spurned and heart-broken God. "But the Lord is the living, the eternal King. When He is angry, the earth trembles; the nations cannot endure His wrath."[25] Despite our technology and medical advances, we are all destined to die and face the judgment of God.[26]

When God moves and calls this world into account, all the power and position in the world will be as putty. Kings, princes, generals, the rich, the mighty and the slave who have rejected God will be reduced to whimpering cowards crying for even the mountains to fall on them and hide them from the day of wrath.[27]

---

[20]Acts 5:1-11
[21]Acts 12:19-23
[22]Hebrews 10:31
[23]Ephesians 4:6; Romans 11:36
[24]Matthew 24:37-39; Luke 17:26-27
[25]Jeremiah 10:10
[26]Hebrews 9:27; II Corinthians 5:10; Revelation 20:11-15
[27]Revelation 6:15-17

However, the all-seeing eyes of God have a much more elevated purpose than noting the evils of humanity, for they continuously search for those who will obey Him and love Him. He has blessings to give and He *will* give them.[28] Some have suggested that the torrential rains which fell at the flood were really the teardrops of a broken-hearted God. But through His dismay and disgust, He still saw clearly. He saw Noah and his family.

GOD'S VIEW OF THOSE WHO TURN TO HIM

Noah believed in God. When God said that a flood was coming so he should build an ark, Noah in deep reverence got busy building.[29] His wife, sons and daughters-in-law did likewise and God graciously saved them from the flood's devastation.[30] Adam had once named all the animals. Now Noah scampered about gathering a pair of each for the renewed earth[31]... and a few extras to offer as sacrifices to God.[32] God is to be remembered, and to be served. And God remembered Noah,[33] and He remembers every individual who turns back to Him.

King Manasseh was a catastrophe. He made a total mess of his long rulership of ancient Judah.[34] He made his people worse than the heathen around them.[35] And God acted. Assyria overran them and Manasseh was shackled and led by a nose-hook. Old and broken, he suddenly humbled himself before the God he had scorned. He pleaded for mercy, and the Lord was moved by his entreaty and listened to his plea.[36] It is easy to touch the great heart of God. He

---

[28]James 1:17

[29]Hebrews 11:7; Genesis 6:12-22

[30]Genesis 6:18; I Peter 3:20-21

[31]Genesis   6:19-21;   7:14-16

[32]Genesis 7:2-3; 8:20-21

[33]Genesis 8:1

[34]II Chronicles 33:1-9

[35]II Chronicles 33:9

[36]II Chronicles 33:10-13

can never resist humble hands which reach out from a contrite and broken heart.[37]

Jonah was sent to cry out against wicked Nineveh: "forty more days and Nineveh will be overturned".[38] Jonah didn't want to warn them because he wanted to see these hated Assyrians go up in smoke like Sodom and Gomorrah. He was afraid to proclaim his warnings, for they might change and spoil Jonah's pleasure at seeing them annihilated. He knew God's heart well enough to know that God is "gracious and compassionate, slow to anger and abounding in love" and that He is "a God who relents from sending calamity".[39] Sure enough, the King of Nineveh got down off his throne and donned sackcloth and sat in ashes, and God saw and had compassion.[40]

"See, I set before you today life and prosperity, death and destruction."[41] The choice is ours, and the power of God is awesomely displayed whichever way we choose. He loves us too passionately to ignore us. "But for those who are self-seeking and who reject the truth and follow evil, there will be wrath and anger. There will be trouble and distress for every human being who does evil."[42] But "He rewards those who earnestly seek Him".[43] "Repent! Turn away from all your offenses... get a new heart and a new spirit. Why will you die... for I have no pleasure in the death of anyone, declares the Sovereign Lord. Repent and live!"[44]

---

[37]Psalm 51:17; Psalm 34:18; Isaiah 66:2; Isaiah 57:15; Matthew 5:3-4
[38]Jonah 1:1-2; 3:1-4
[39]Jonah 4:1-3
[40]Jonah 3:5-10
[41]Deuteronomy 30:15
[42]Romans 2:8-9
[43]Hebrews 11:6
[44]Ezekiel 18:30-32

1. How intensive is God's concern for the world He created? Discuss.

2. How many of the details of your life are on the mind and heart of God? Discuss.

3. What is the impact on your life of knowing the eyes of God are always on you?

4. How could God bring a flood to destroy His creation if He loved them?

5. What is the objective of all of God's acts of discipline?

6. Why do people doubt the flood account?

7. What seems to be the thing God is looking for most?

8. What was so vital in the reprieves received by King Manasseh and the people of Nineveh?

9. Why is indifference never a characteristic of God?

Notes

4   THE FATHER FINDS A SPECIAL FRIEND

God is all-sufficient, we proclaim: He does not need our time, talents or money. He does not need our praise. He does not need us, but we need Him.

I am not sure what all God might need, but I am confident that He deeply wants a number of things. Above all He seems to want to be with us, to have fellowship with us. He came in the evening for His daily rendezvous in the Garden of Eden with the man and woman he had lovingly created. "Where are you?" He asked in obvious disappointment.[1] When rebellion and degradation ravaged humanity, He sought out Noah and his family to save. He provided for them. He remembered them. He blessed them.[2]

Satan stalks the earth, his eyes straining to find those he can pounce on and destroy.[3]   God's eyes also constantly scan His creation, looking for those whose hearts are turned to Him and who need His help and encouragement.[4]

Something in the awesome nature of God finds its fulfillment in enjoying nearness to His creatures who bear His own image. God is love,[5] and His love is expressed in graciousness, compassion, kindness and generosity. But what are these if there is no one upon whom to lavish them? Perhaps His very nature makes essential our existence.

With such eyes and such a heart, He was bound to find Abraham. Abraham needed God. God wanted Abraham. Great things were sure to happen... and they did.

---

[1] Genesis 3:8-9
[2] Genesis 6:18-21; 8:1; 9:1
[3] Job 1:6-7; I Peter 5:8
[4] II Chronicles 16:9; Psalm 46:1
[5] I John 4:8-16

25

As a young man, Abraham got a good boost from his earthly father Terah (and children need and deserve this kind of boost). Most likely at God's urging, Terah decided to move his family from corrupt Ur of the Chaldeans. Ur was in the same area of the world as ancient Babylon. There the ungrateful descendants of the survivors of the flood gathered to forget God and build a massive memorial to themselves. It was there that God multiplied their languages.[6] In time, some of them built a great walled city and a powerful empire. They invented new gods for themselves, gods who were like themselves, and they became entrenched in corruption. Terah had had enough. He headed to a new place called Canaan. Good for Terah!

But he never made it. About halfway there, he settled in Haran. So the voice of God spoke again, this time to Terah's son Abraham. "Leave your country, your people and your father's household and go to the land I will show you."[7] He called Abraham to leave a comfortable house, the security of family and friends, and to become a nomad living in a tent in a strange land.[8] He promised to make of Abraham a great nation, to bless his name and all his offspring, and to give his descendents a new land.[9] Would you trade a solid home, family and security for a string of promises? Abraham did, because he knew God and believed in Him thoroughly.[10] God likes this. He likes this a lot.

AN EXCITING ADVENTURE WITH GOD

So Abraham journeyed for days, weeks, months... a youthful man of 75, with his beautiful wife Sarah, and tag-along nephew Lot. All along the way he left a telltail trail of his reverence and love for God - altars where he offered his affections to his God.[11]

---

[6] Genesis 11:1-9
[7] Genesis 12:1
[8] Hebrews 11:8-9
[9] Genesis 12:2-7
[10] Hebrews 11:8-10
[11] Genesis 12:7,8; 13:4,18

Constantly God came to Abraham to talk things over; to restate His promises; to reassure him.[12] God was constantly on Abraham's mind. And Abraham was on God's. Here was one who believed in Him, listened to Him, and loved Him. So God constantly watched over Abraham and got Abraham out of difficulties...difficulties of Abraham's own doing. Twice Abraham lied about his beautiful wife while on their travels and got himself into hot water. Both times God bailed him out.[13] God had said to "leave your people" but Abraham allowed Lot to come along; a troublesome mistake for Abraham. First there was a quarrel between Lot's shepherds and Abraham's. Like God, Abraham disliked dissension. He gave Lot the choice of relocation sites and Lot selfishly grabbed what looked best.[14] Then the vexing Lot got too close to sinful Sodom and was captured in a power-struggle battle between local kings. Abraham, at his own expense and risk, assembled a 318-man army and rescued Lot, along with a sizable bundle of stolen goods.[15] Sodom was delighted to have their stolen citizens returned and offered Abraham all the goods as a just reward. But Abraham said, "I have raised my hand to the Lord, God Most High, Creator of heaven and earth". He refused to accept one shred of the goods lest someone would say "I made Abraham rich".[16] For he wanted the world to know that his wonderful God, and He alone, was responsible for all Abraham had or was. We today should be so insightful. To God be the glory.

On his travel home from the raid, Abraham met the enigmatic Melchizedek, an early priest to the Most High God. He immediately sensed the presence of God in Abraham and knew God had given him victory. So Abraham freely gave ten percent of the goods to this man of God.[17] It was easy to give to God for God had given so much to him.

---

[12]Genesis 12:7; 13:14-17; 15:1ff; 17:1ff; 18:1ff
[13]Genesis 12:10-20; 20:1-18
[14]Genesis 13:5-11
[15]Genesis 14:1-24
[16]Genesis 14:22-23
[17]Genesis 14:18-20; Hebrews 7:1-10

The communication and communion between God and Abraham remained the immovable center of Abraham's life. Time had passed and the promise of abundant descendents grew dimmer. Sarah was childless. So God and Abraham talked it over.[18] Abraham suggested to God that since no children had been born, he should designate an heir to his possessions. After all, old age was creeping in. It looked impossible, but God said Abraham would have a son born of his own body. "Can you count the stars?" God asked. Abraham couldn't count them; nor can we. "So shall your offspring be," God announced The odds may have seemed slim to no chance at all, but God had said it and that was enough for Abraham. He simply believed Him, knowing it would happen because God had said so; you can trust God. And God was delighted. He loves it when someone just believes Him and acts on their trust in Him. God was impressed and recorded this moment for everyone to note and imitate.[19]

Abraham was not a larger-than-life hero; he was a weak human being who believed his God. He allowed his beloved wife Sarah to talk him into a foolish scheme. He was to have a baby by her maidservant Hagar, as a substitute for her own childlessness. Abraham went along with this plan and Ishmael was born, thus creating a furor in his household which still survives today in the relentless tension between Arabs and Israelites.[20] But God in his love took care of the now ill-favored Hagar and her son.

Abraham walked with God and the years rolled past. Soon he was nearly 100 years old and Sarah was almost 90.[21] Child-bearing was now a physical impossibility for them both.[22] And again God came to discuss things with Abraham.[23] "I am God Almighty" He

---

[18]Genesis 15:1-6

[19]Romans 4:1-3ff; Galatians 3:6-9ff

[20]Genesis 16:1-15

[21]Genesis 17:1,17; Romans 4:19

[22]Romans 4:18-19

[23]Genesis 17:1-22 - God announced He was El Shaddai (Hebrew) :God Almighty

proclaimed. How Abraham needed to believe this now. How Almighty was God? God let him know the time had come at last. Time to fulfill His promises. Time to change his name from one which meant "exalted Father" to one which meant "father of many". He was to be the father of a nation... very fruitful. But Abraham and Sarah were too old. However, they were not too old for God.

GOD KEEPS PROMISES

And Abraham simply believed God, like he had always believed God. He fell down in laughter and said, "can this be?" Everyone laughed.[24] Even the son to be born would have the name Isaac which means "he laughs". Three mysterious visitors arrived at their tent and were offered warm hospitality. Abraham saw God in these men.[25] Abraham saw God in everything good. They announced to this barren couple the best news of all... the same news which came centuries later to the desperate Zechariah and Elizabeth.[26] "Is anything too hard for the Lord?'[27] After nine months, a son would be born, and indeed he was. What a source of joy for them both! How God keeps His promises![28]

But it was headache time again. Lot was still living in the Sodom environ and Sodom, along with Gomorrah, was on a list to be destroyed by God. God was tired of their arrogance, self-indulgence and lack of concern for her poor and needy.[29] This presented a problem to God. So He asked, "Shall I hide from Abraham what I am about to do?"[30] A natural response to this would be that God can do whatever He desires without consulting anyone. He is, after all, God. But Abraham was special because he was listening to God and obeying God and really trusting God. He was to become a great nation and to serve as a powerful witness for God throughout

---

[24]Genesis 17:17; 18:12

[25]Genesis 18:1-15

[26]Luke 1:13

[27]Genesis 18:14

[28]Romans 4:18-25

[29]Ezekiel 16:49-50

[30]Genesis 18:17

the ages.[31] He was chosen to lead his family and succeeding generations in doing what was right before God.[32] The parallels between Abraham and anyone today who decides to act in complete trust of the Lord are striking. God is ready to pronounce His righteousness on any one today who believes in Him and the Son whom He sent and He will make this one a special ambassador of His.[33] Not just for Abraham but "for us who believe in Him who raised Jesus from the dead". We are no less called and chosen than he.[34]

Now Abraham had his long awaited son. The promise of God had been kept. Nothing could separate Abraham and his precious son, Isaac. Or could it? The voice of God speaks once more. "Take your son, your only son, Isaac, whom you love, and go... sacrifice him there as a burnt offering...[35] Certainly it was easier to have left home, family and friends than to offer up his beloved son. This was too much! But we read no words of protest. Abraham was up early the next morning on a death march with his son. For three days they trudged along and finally the boy was secured to the altar and the knife raised. How could Abraham do it? He again simply trusted God. This was the son of promise and the link to the great nation and all God's promises to Abraham. God would handle it -- Abraham must simply believe and obey. In his heart he thought of his Almighty Father and reasoned that God would raise Isaac from the dead.[36]

HOW CLOSE CAN A PERSON BE WITH GOD?

What a relationship Abraham had with God...and God with Abraham. Abraham believed God. He knew God was Almighty. He revered God above all else. He obeyed God. And in return, God greatly blessed Abraham. But there seems to be even more here. God has a deep respect for Abraham. He constantly explains

---

[31]Genesis 18:18; Romans 4
[32]Genesis 18:19
[33]Romans 4:22-25; II Corinthians 5:20
[34]Romans 8:28-30; Ephesians 1:4-6; I Corinthians 1:9
[35]Genesis 22:2-19
[36]Hebrews 11:19

things to him. He will not act upon Lot's Sodom until Abraham is consulted.[37] He even allows Abraham to reverently debate with Him over the number of righteous ones required to save the city.[38] The fact is, the astounding and unbelievable fact is, that Abraham and God were friends.[39]

"Abraham believed God, and it was credited to him as righteousness. And he was called God's friend."[40] A new dimension of God is revealed. A most exciting dimension. He desires us to fear and reverence Him as Abraham did.[41] He expects us to show our faith in Him by unflinching obedience to His will.[42] But He also longs to make us His intimate friends. Imagine that, to be the friend of God!

We thought God only wanted unquestioning, knee-bending servants. But He has always wanted much more. He has much more than this to give. He wants friends. Friends who know what He is doing and love Him and who have close fellowship with Him.[43] Praise be to our Father who has called us into fellowship with Himself, with His glorious Son,[44] and with His comforting Holy Spirit.

---

[37]Genesis   18:16-21
[38]Genesis   18:23-33
[39]Isaiah 41:8; II Chronicles 20:7
[40]James 2:23
[41]Genesis 22:12; Proverbs 1:7; Philippians 2:12-13; Revelation 14:7
[42]I Samuel 15:22-23; James 2:21-22
[43]John 15:13-15; John 14:23; I John 1:3-4
[44]I Corinthians 1:9

1. What indications do the scriptures give that God has a genuine need for relationship with us?

2. What action did Terah begin which Abraham carried to fulfillment?

3. Would it be difficult to leave all past ties and travel to a totally new location? What about in Abraham's day?

4. What problems did Abraham have with Lot? How did Abraham reflect God's nature in dealing with these?

5. Discuss the constant communication that went on between God and Abraham.

6. What attitude of Abraham's continued to deeply impress God? Why?

7. Why did God feel compelled to discuss Sodom with Abraham?

8. What characteristics in God's and Abraham's relationship show friendship?

9. How can we secure the friendship of God today?

King David was a great lover. He had a great love for nature.[1] and a special sensitivity to people around him.[2] But he had an unusual love affair. He passionately loved the law of the Lord.[3] The poets have given us their praise songs, and so we have odes to the west wind, to evening, to a nightingale and even on a Grecian urn. But David's heart poured out what we might call "An Ode to the Law of the Lord". The shorter version is Psalm 19:7-14 and the much longer is the epic Psalm 119.

A ROMANTIC KING WHO LOVED GOD'S LAW

We all would agree with David that God's law is perfect, trustworthy, right, radiant, pure and sure,[4] but how many of us would describe it as "more precious than pure gold" or "sweeter than the honeycomb"?[5] After all, a law, even God's law, simply states what you can and cannot do. It marks out the boundaries and identifies your failures. Even as I am writing, my ten year old daughter is practicing piano with a metronome. It ticks out its relentless rhythm. It adds nothing to the music. It only reveals when she is off the beat and demands she "get with it".

David's praise arises not so much from admiration for the force and logic or even the completeness of God's law, but for the great rewards which always come to those who walk in God's law.[6] David loved life and realized that in keeping God's law life reaches its highest potential. He saw in the law an expression of the

---

[1] Psalm 8:3-8; 19:1-6
[2] I Samuel 18:1ff; 22:20-23; 24:1-7; 25:32-34; II Samuel 3:31-34; 9:1-13; 16:5-14
[3] Psalm 119:48, 97
[4] Psalm 19:7-9
[5] Psalm 19:10; 119:103,127
[6] Psalm 19:11

wonderful God who gave this life-sustaining code. He saw the love of God and was stirred to obey these decrees.[7] David saw the law as not just giving direction to his life but as that which revived his soul, made him wise, gave joy to his heart and light to his eyes.[8]

But David didn't dream this up on some pastoral hillside. He learned it from long hours of diligent study of God's writings[9] and from the experiences of his life.[10] You should take time now to turn and read the Bible's longest chapter, Psalm 119. Observe closely David's love affair with God and His law. He wouldn't trade God's law for all the money in the world.[11] He stands in awe before the law.[12] With God's law sustaining him, he pauses frequently each day to praise God for His righteous laws.[13] "Let me live that I may praise You" David cries.[14]

David learned another great truth as well Law does not really bind our lives or limit our pleasures. It is the cornerstone of all freedom.[15] Peace and freedom were Adam's and Eve's in the garden. Difficulties, bondage and death came when they disobeyed God's law.[16] Exactly the same is true today. Where the Spirit of the Lord is, there is freedom.[17] Freedom from being controlled by one's own passions and lusts.[18] Freedom from hurting people. Freedom to become all we were designed by God to be. No limitations. The sky and beyond is the limit.[19]

---

[7]Psalm   119:64,88

[8]Psalm   19:7-8

[9]Psalm   119:15-16,20,48,55,62,97,99,164

[10]Psalm   119:26,35,56,59,67,71,100,152:   Psalm   37:25

[11]Psalm   119:72

[12]Psalm   119:120

[13]Psalm   119:164

[14]Psalm   119:175

[15]Psalm 119:32,45; John 8:32,36; James 1:25; 2:12-13

[16]Genesis   2:16-17; 3:16-19,23; Romans 6:16-23

[17]II Corinthians 3:17

[18]Titus 3:3-5ff; Galatians 5:16-18,24

[19]Ephesians 1:3; 2:10; 3:19

God did not give the law to curb human accomplishment and fulfillment. He did not attempt to curtail human enjoyment. He is the one who gave us these grand capacities. Rather, He gave us law to protect us from each other, to keep us from over-working our employees,[20] to hinder us from murdering, stealing, lying and sexually abusing one another,[21] to show us how to treat our parents and thus to make our own lives go as they should,[22] and to center our heart and minds on the good God who created and maintains our lives.[23]

The law was given as a tangible and fixed reminder that God is good and that we are to be like God -- good.[24] Good to one another and to ourselves. Over and over He proclaimed that His people were to do such and such because "I am the Lord"[25] They were to live right and not hurt people, they were to help the poor, the orphans and widows, and take care of their bodies, because He was the Lord and they were the people who wore His name.[26] Their lifestyles were to reflect the character of the God who directed and blessed them. They were His living witnesses to show Him to the nations around them.[27] Only by obeying His laws, which reflected His very nature, could this be accomplished.

God knew that without this central focus on Him through His laws, His people would soon turn to idols and would be doing all kinds of

---

[20]Exodus 20:8-11; Mark 2:27

[21]Exodus 20:13-17; I Thessalonians 4:3-8

[22]Exodus 20:12; Ephesians 6:1-3

[23]Exodus 20:1-7

[24]Psalm 119:68

[25]Leviticus 18:2,5,21; 19:2-3,12,14,16,18,25,28,30,31,32,34,35,37,etc.

[26]Genesis 32:28; II Chronicles 7:14

[27]Isaiah 43:10-13; 44:6-8

35

monstrous things. Things such as forcing their children to pass through sacrificial fires to appease Molech.[28]

God viewed His law as a way to draw His people closer to Himself. He revealed Himself as a God who was near to them and heard their prayers. They were a fortunate people to have a God who gave them such fair and righteous laws.[29] Taken into their hearts and lives, these decrees and commands would assure that the only true God was with them and that His laws would guarantee them a good and long life in the land God had given them.[30] He revealed His feelings when He said, "Oh, that their hearts would be inclined to fear Me and keep all My commands always, so that it may go well with them and their children forever".[31] The law was a part of the Lord's great plan of discipline to bring His people to joyful maturity and to a place of bubbling streams, beautiful valleys and unprecedented prosperity.[32] God disciplines so that He will have people to whom He can safely give abundant blessings. He did so then, and He does today.[33]

God called a people and gave them a law at Mt. Sinai,[34] but at the same time he made a covenant with them,[35] one brimming with magnificent promises. For several centuries He blessed them despite their failure to really trust and obey Him, and even when they were on the brink of destruction due to their excessive disobedience, God expressed His enduring plans and desires for His "people of the law". He states, "For I know My plans I have for you... plans to prosper you and not harm you, plans to give you hope and a future. Then you will call upon Me and come and pray to Me, and I will listen to you. You will seek Me and find Me when you seek Me with all your heart. I will be found of you...and will

---

[28]Leviticus 18:21; 20:2-5; II Kings 23:10; Jeremiah 19:5
[29]Deuteronomy 4:5-8
[30]Deuteronomy 4:39-40
[31]Deuteronomy 5:29,33
[32]Deuteronomy 8:1-9
[33]Hebrews 12:5-11
[34]Exodus 19:23-20:21
[35]Exodus 24:1-8

bring you back from captivity."[36] Again He says, "I will never stop doing good to them...I will rejoice in doing them good and will assuredly plant them in this land with all My heart and soul."[37]

God never intended His law to be a dry set of rules or a burdensome weight on the backs of His people. He had Moses tell His people at the beginning, "Take to heart all the words I have solemnly declared to you this day, so that you may command your children to obey carefully all the word of this law. They are not just idle words for you -- they are your life."[38]

WHAT IS THE PLACE OF LAW TODAY?

But why all this study of the law since we today are not under the law but under grace?[39] One reason is that from the law we see some important aspects of the complex character of God. Another reason is that for hundreds of years this law was a great tutor-teacher to Israel to bring them to Christ Jesus[40] yet we so often misunderstand the concept of God and law today.

God knew that not even His law could establish and maintain a person in relationship with Him[41] and relationship is what God desires.[42] The only way a law system could sustain a relationship between a person and God is if that person could keep the law perfectly,[43] yet no one but Jesus Christ ever has or ever will. God's law shows just how imperfect and sinful we really are.[44] Instead of bringing us life, it actually became an instrument of death.[45] God's law taught us that His righteousness was beyond

---

[36]Jeremiah   29:11-14

[37]Jeremiah   32:36-41

[38]Deuteronomy   32:46-47

[39]Romans 6:14-15; Galatians 5:18

[40]Galatians 3:24-25

[41]Galatians 2:15-16; 3:10-11; Romans 3:19-20

[42]Leviticus 26:2-13; II Corinthians 6:16-18

[43]Galatians 3:10-14; John   7:19

[44]Romans 3:19-20; 7:13

[45]Romans 7:8-10; 6:23; I Corinthians 15:56

our grasp. We stand condemned and hopeless before Him. But by our faith in Christ Jesus He has given us victory over sin and death.[46]

We will notice more about the victory in Jesus Christ in later lessons, but for now we want to learn about our Father by observing His use of law in our lives. We seem by nature to be both repulsed (we want to be free to do as we desire) and drawn to a law system. We want cut and dry directions for our lives. And we want it simple. But life and relationships are not simple; they are most complex. And Christianity is foundationally relationships. Since we often long for a simplified law, we may create one where none exists. This is what the Pharisees did, and what many do today.

Some seem to feel that the law of Moses was taken away[47] and in its place came the law of Christ.[48] If one could not keep the law of Moses, then the law of Christ can be nothing short of a holy terror. Moses said that you shouldn't commit adultery, but Jesus condemned even looking lustfully at a woman.[49] The law condemned murder, but Jesus condemned hostile anger.[50] Who can measure up to the perfect Son of God?

A careful study of the New Testament will reveal that the "law of Christ" is not a new set of rules and commands consisting of a set number of acts of worship or steps to salvation. It is not a new law code. The law of Christ is the royal law to love.[51] We are not bound to the Mosaic law code. Nor are we now obliged to establish and maintain our relationship with God on the merit of our good works.[52]

---

[46]Romans 3:21-26; I Corinthians 15:57; Galatians 3:13-14
[47]Ephesians 2:14-15; Colossians 2:13-14
[48]Galatians 6:2
[49]Matthew 5:27-28
[50]Matthew 5:21-22
[51]James 2:8; Leviticus 19:18; Galatians 5:14; Romans 13:8-10
[52]Romans 4:4-5; Ephesians 2:3-10; II Timothy 1:9; Titus 3:4-5

We are called to the highest standard of relationship. We are to love God and our fellow man above all else.[53] We are freed from law which we can never keep to grace which can empower us to obey.[54] Knowing God and His nature, we know that all the good required by God's law is to be the cornerstone of our lives. We are empowered not by an external law but by His own Spirit[55] which abides in our hearts. He does for us what we could never do, because our trust is in our Father and His Son.[56]

We are the special creation of God; His new creation.[57] We are His workmanship.[58] The Greek word for workmanship is "poema" -- our word for poem. We are God's poem... and may we be a poem which continually praises God. One which does the good works for which we were recreated.

---

[53]Matthew 22:34-40
[54]Romans 6:14-18
[55]Ephesians 1:15-19; 3:14-21; I Corinthians 6:19-20
[56]Romans 8:1-17
[57]II Corinthians 5:17; Galatians 6:15
[58]Ephesians 2:10

1. What seems to be the strongest feeling which David has for God's law?

2. What did David understand about the relationship between law and freedom?

3. How does disobeying God take away freedom?

4. When people stop focusing on God, what happens to their lives?

5. What did God hope His law would do in the lives of His people, Israel?

6. Why should we study the law today?

7. Does the law of God bring us relationship and life?

8. What is the highest law or standard by which one can live?

9. Since we are God's new creation, what is to be happening in our lives?

You could say Moses spent the first 40 years of his life with a silver spoon in his mouth, the second 40 years with a shepherd's staff in his hand, and the last 40 years with a big pain in the neck. Actually, he was fortunate to have even lived one year on the earth, for he was born in a Hebrew home which was part of the enslaved nation of Israel.[1] Egypt, their master, had grown afraid of Israel's growth, so all male babies of the Hebrews were to be drowned in the Nile river.[2]

But the Hebrew midwives bravely defied the orders of the Pharaoh; and God, moved by these brave women, blessed them richly.[3] So Moses' life was spared. Then his mother took over. After keeping him hidden for three months,[4] she laid him in a basket and placed it in the Nile. Trusting God, she saw her beloved boy adopted by the royal princess and herself placed in charge as his nurse.[5] Moses must have heard this great story over and over. As he grew up in luxury he was aware he was really one of the Hebrews who were enslaved.[6]

Finally one day his "Hebrewness" took over. In an outburst he killed an oppressive Egyptian guard and was forced to flee Egypt. He had forfeited a rich future to stand with his own.[7] The book of Hebrews tells us Moses acted by faith.[8] He believed in the true and

---

[1] Exodus 1:6-14

[2] Exodus 1:15-22

[3] Exodus 1:20-21

[4] Exodus 2:1-2; Acts 7:20

[5] Exodus 2:5-10; Hebrews 11:23; Acts 7:21-22

[6] Exodus 11:24-25; Acts 7:22

[7] Exodus 2:11-15; Acts 7:23-29

[8] Hebrews 11:24,27,28

living God. Better to obey God and take what He had to offer than to rely on Egyptian treasures.[9] We can learn much from this man.

As Moses fled, he came to Midian. Already cast as a rescuer, he came to the aid of some mistreated shepherd girls, and for his gallantry, one became his wife.[10] For 40 years he lived the relatively peaceful life of a shepherd. Two sons were born and much thinking must have taken place.[11] Why had his life been dramatically spared? Why had he grown up learning all the great mysteries of Egypt? Why was he given the long "inside view" of the royal leadership? How could all this help a mere Midianite shepherd? But God can always use an education, any education, for His purposes... if we will let Him.

A burning bush just kept burning. And burning. Moses drew near and heard a startling voice. "Moses, Moses!"[12] Moses was told to take off his shoes for the ground was holy with the Lord's presence. Wherever the Lord is found is holy ground. Moses was rightfully overwhelmed and hid his face from the awesome God.[13] Moses had heard about God back in Egypt and believed. He had meditated upon God and surely prayed often to Him on the grassy hillsides of Midian. But now, here He was.

God did not identify Himself as the God of creation or the God of the universe. "I am the God of Abraham... Isaac ... Jacob."[14] God is the God of people; His identity is defined by the people with whom He has relationships.[15] Abraham had been his friend[16] and

---

9 Hebrews   11:25-26

10 Exodus   2:15-21

11 Exodus 2:22; Acts 7:29-30

12 Exodus 3:1-4; Acts 7:30-31

13 Exodus 3:5-6; Acts 7:33

14 Exodus 3:6; Acts 7:32

15 Exodus 3:6

16 Isaiah 41:8; II Chronicles 20:7; James 2:23

42

God wanted to be understood in the light of that beautiful relationship. "I am the God of Abraham" He says repeatedly.[17]

Moses, now a prepared man, was called by God to return to Egypt to lead God's people from bondage.[18] God cared deeply for His people and wanted them free.[19] He still does. Moses was taken aback by this request. The quiet pastures were inviting. The rescuer of old was suddenly subdued. He offered four compelling arguments for not going.First, he was a "nobody" shepherd; who would listen to him?[20] Second, he would never be able to explain who God was in the strange land of Egypt.[21] Then, he was sure they would never believe God had sent him.[22] And finally, Moses suggested that he couldn't talk in front of people - he was no orator, only a shepherd.[23]

God's answers came back straight and convincing. "I will be with you."[24] "I Am who I Am... I Am has sent you."[25] "What is that in your hand?"[26] "Who gave man his mouth...go, I will help you speak and teach you what to say."[27] God had answers for all Moses' questions and excuses. God has all the answers today also.

Moses' true colors of the moment then came through. He said, "O Lord, please send someone else to do it."[28] He simply didn't want to go. Now God's patience turned to anger. Problems He can deal

---

[17]Exodus 3:6, 15, 16: 4:5; Psalm 47:9; Matthew 22:32; Mark 12:26; Like 20:37; Acts 7:32
[18]Exodus 3:9-10; Acts 7:34
[19]Exodus 3:7-10
[20]Exodus 3:11
[21]Exodus 3:13
[22]Exodus 4:1
[23]Exodus 4:10
[24]Exodus 3:112
[25]Exodus 3:14
[26]Exodus 4:2
[27]Exodus 4:11-12
[28]Exodus 4:13

with and overcome; refusal is another matter. God is God. He is not to be said "no" to. God gave Moses his brother Aaron to help him and sent him on his way. Excuse time was over. God had spoken; now it was time to move![29]

With God's prevailing help, Moses was able to overcome strong Egyptian resistance and free the 600,000 men plus women and children who composed Israel.[30] Moses' unwavering faith in God lead the frightened and "turn back now" horde into the wilderness[31] Soon they were to march into the promised land where all would be wonderful, but the people were full of fear which was revealed in frequent and widespread murmuring and often overt rebellion. Moses was leading a kicking, foot-dragging stubborn mule of a people. The task seemed impossible.[32]

After Moses delivered to them the new law and covenant, they seemed ready to trust God.[33] But a 40 day stay on Mt. Sinai by Moses brought out the worst in the people. They flagrantly disobeyed God's newly established law and turned to idols.[34] Now Moses took up in earnest a new role, one he had actually begun earlier; he became their mediator.[35] When God announced that Israel should perish and that a new nation from Moses' descendents would take its place,[36] Moses pleaded for his people and called on God to spare the people He had so brilliantly rescued. "Remember your servants Abraham, Isaac, and Israel. You promised them a great nation and a land."[37]

God did remember and the people were spared. However, Moses had now risen to a new position, and it was a most difficult one.

---

[29]Exodus 4:14-17
[30]Exodus chapters 5-12; Acts 7:35-36; Hebrews 11:29
[31]Acts 7:39
[32]Exodus chapters 13-19
[33]Exodus 24:1-11
[34]Exodus 24:12-18; 32:1-8
[35]Exodus 20:18-21; Galatians 3:19-20
[36]Exodus 32:9-10
[37]Exodus 32:11-14

Not only must he lead these stubborn people, but he must stand for them before God; he must speak for them, and he felt the enormity of the task. How could he ever stand up under such awesome responsibility?

A tent of meeting was erected where Moses would come and meet with the people and deal with their problems,[38] but more significantly, God would come here to meet with Moses. He came, not as a distant potentate or even an imposing divine King, but to meet with Moses "face to face, as a man speaks with his friend".[39] So... God has another friend! An amazing God...He does not want stooping and posturing servants, He wants loving and cooperative friends. He wants to meet us face to face, to help us, and bless us.[40]

Moses felt that his time was up. With God's help, He had done all he could do. He needed more. But more what? More of God! He speaks face to face with God. He says that God has been telling him to lead these people but he feels he lacks something, something vital. Even though God had been powerfully with Moses all along, Moses now says, "If you are pleased with me, teach me Your ways so I may know You and continue to find favor with You".[41] God did not say "you already know Me. Remember the plagues; remember the Red Sea and the manna.". He understood Moses' need, the need for a deeper grasp of God. The need to know that God was actually walking with, maybe even in, him. He must truly and deeply know God. Here today lies our greatest single need.

"Now show me Your glory," Moses entreats,[42] but he has asked the impossible. Who can look upon God in all His glory and live?[43] Yet God is entirely open with His beloved friend Moses. He would not call on Moses to perform great tasks and not fully equip him (and so it is with us today as well). God gently explained that Moses could not physically look on His glorious face and live. Yet God could

---

[38] Exodus 33:7-10

[39] Exodus 33:11

[40] Hebrews 4:14-16

[41] Exodus 33:12-13

[42] Exodus 33:18

[43] Genesis 32:30; Isaiah 6:5

meet his request. He would cause all His goodness to pass in front of him and He would proclaim His matchless name and reveal the full extent of His nature.[44] He would also show him as much physically as a human could take in.[45]

The next day Moses busied himself chiseling out the new stone tablets[46] but he must have been on pins and needles of excitement. Then God came and passed in front of Moses and told him just exactly what He was like. "The Lord, the Lord, the compassionate and gracious God, slow to anger, abounding in love and faithfulness, maintaining love to thousands, and forgiving wickedness, rebellion and sin . Yet He does not leave the guilty unpunished; He punishes the children and their children for the sin of the fathers to the third and fourth generation."[47]

Now Moses knew God. He knew what He was like. He could ponder all these characteristics and know that this God could bring even rebellious Israel to the promised land. Even if it took 40 years.[48] Moses could endure unbelievable complaining,[49] open opposition and treason[50] and even harsh criticism from his own brother and sister.[51]

Moses stood face to face with God. They were friends. And all this made Moses the most humble man on the earth.[52] Being close to God always has that effect. It never makes one prideful or arrogant.

Moses was not perfect; He stumbled at Kadesh and was not allowed to enter the promised land.[53] (He had likely had enough of

---

[44]Exodus   33:19-20
[45]Exodus   33:21-23
[46]Exodus   34:1-4
[47]Exodus   34:5-7
[48]Acts 7:36; Numbers   14:1-35
[49]Numbers   Chapters   11-14, 20;   I Corinthians   10:1-11
[50]Numbers   16:1-35
[51]Numbers   12:1-16
[52]Numbers   12:3
[53]Numbers   20:1-12, 24;   Deuteronomy   1:37;   3:27;   34:1-4

troublesome Israel anyway.) So he died at age 120 with clear eyes and a strong body. Life had been good with God. It always is. Then God buried His old friend. God is always right there when those who have made Him their friend die.[54] He wants to be right there to take them home to live with Him forever.[55] Our Father is a great friend.[56]

---

[54]Deuteronomy 34:5-8
[55]Psalm 116:15
[56]John 5:28-29; 14:1-3; I John 5:13

1. In what areas do we need to imitate Moses' rejection of a life of comfort in Egypt?

2. How did heroic women greatly affect the survival of Moses?

3. Do we today ever stand on "holy ground"? When or where?

4. What is the significance of the statement "I am the God of Abraham?

5. What excuses do we often make today and how does God answer them?

6. Moses had experienced God's power over and over, yet he desired more. What did he seek? What about us today?

7. What is God really like? How does this affect your life?

8. What effect does standing near to God always have on a person?

9. Where was God when Moses died? Where is God today when we die?

People in ancient times did not have mirrors hanging in every room. In fact, polished mirrors were quite rare. The only reflections one caught of oneself were the hazy images cast by a pond or lake. In the person of David we have a human reflection of the heart of God; not a perfect reflection, only a rather hazy resemblance. However, from David's life we can learn some valuable things about the great nature of God.

David was a man with a heart deeply stamped by the character of God. As God Himself records, David was a man after God's own heart.[1], and God has always been big into hearts. God knows that the heart ultimately controls everything. It is life's wellspring out of which all life flows.[2] God needed a new king for Israel for Saul's heart had gone bad.[3] God sought someone with a heart like His own.[4] His ambassador, Samuel, and Jesse the father, agreed Eliab was the one.[5] He looked like a king. God however, had other plans. "The Lord does not look at the things man looks at. Man looks at the outward appearance, but the Lord looks at the heart."[6] So the shepherd boy David was chosen.[7]

WHAT'S SO SPECIAL ABOUT THIS SHEPHERD'S HEART

Though he was the anointed king, his reign had to wait for the right time. Meanwhile, David served the present (though rejected) king Saul[8] as a harp player and singer. But soon he heard the defiant

---

[1] I Samuel 13::14; Acts 13:22
[2] Proverbs 4:23; Matthew 12:34; Luke 6:45
[3] I Samuel 15:22-26; 16:14-23
[4] I Samuel 13:14
[5] I Samuel 16:6
[6] I Samuel 16:7
[7] I Samuel 16 ;11-13
[8] I Samuel 16:14-23

insults of the nine-foot tall Goliath. All God's people shivered before him. David was incensed. "Who is this uncircumcised Philistine that he should defy the armies of the living God?"[9] David had the body of a boy but his heart trusted God. The same Lord who delivered him from the lion and bear in the pasture would give him victory over this Philistine.[10] He warned the giant warrior "that it is not by sword or spear that the Lord saves; for the battle is the Lord's."[11] There is a God in Israel[12] and whoever trusts in this God will never come out red faced and defeated.[13] Somewhere in the pasture fields with the sheep, David had learned to love and trust God. And this was enough. It is always enough. And nothing else will do.

A GOOD HEART BATTLES A NASTY ENEMY

Saul was rejected which made him fearful and vindictive. David's continuing successes deepened his fear and jealousy.[14] Amid it all, a beautiful lifelong friendship blossomed between Saul's son, Jonathan, and David. Jonathan was heir apparent to the throne but would never serve. David was anointed to kingship but Jonathan's father stood in his way. Yet friendship and love surpass all obstacles. A love born of God's nature thrived here. A love which can cause potential enemies to love, not out of lust, but out of sacrifice and caring.[15]

David could have stayed and fought and won. He was God's king. But he too deeply respected the Lord's first anointed king, Saul. Instead, David fled for years before the maddened Saul. Twice he could easily have finished off Saul, but he refused,[16] and when Saul fell in battle against Philistia, David did not rejoice; he grieved.

---

[9] I Samuel 17:26
[10] I Samuel 17:34-37
[11] I Samuel 17:47
[12] I Samuel 17:46
[13] Isaiah 28:16; Romans 9:33; 10:11
[14] I Samuel 18:28-29
[15] I Samuel chapters 19-20; esp. 20:17, 23' II Samuel 1:17-27
[16] I Samuel 24:1-6; 26:1-25

"How the mighty have fallen."[17] Strife continued between David's and Saul's camps. Saul's captain, Abner, turned to David but was slain. David again grieved the loss of a great life,[18] even his enemy's life. Then Saul's son, Ishbosheth was murdered. David decried this action.[19] People ready to oppose David were touched by his attitude toward the old regime and its leaders.[20] Much strife was likely averted. Like God, David did not rejoice when bad befell people.[21]

A MAN WHOSE HEART CAN BE TOUCHED

While fleeing Saul, David met an ungrateful Nabal. Though David had likely saved many of Nabal's sheep while camping nearby, Nabal refused hospitality to the bedraggled and hungry army of David. Enraged, David prepared to destroy Nabal's household but Nabal's wife, Abigail, came with food and entreated David to avoid bloodshed he would later regret. David listened and his heart was turned. And he praised Abigail.[22]

Then there was Mephibosheth, Saul's grandson, who was miserably crippled by a terrible fall.[23] He was of the deposed royal family. What could be done with him? David invited him to dinner and then made him a permanent part of his royal household.[24] Mephibosheth said he was as useless as a dead dog, but David gave him land and a position.[25] How like his heavenly Father David was... the helper of the weak and hopeless.[26]

---

[17] II Samuel 1:17-24

[18] II Samuel 3:31-39

[19] II Samuel 4:1-11

[20] II Samuel 3:36-39

[21] Ezekiel 18:32; I Corinthians 13:5-6

[22] I Samuel 25:1-42; esp. vss.32-35

[23] II Samuel 4:4

[24] II Samuel 9:1-13

[25] II Samuel 19:14-30

[26] Deuteronomy 10:17-18; Psalm 10:14; 68:5

David remembered what he learned. It became part of a heart which each year became more patient, understanding and compassionate; more God-like. Later King David was pursued by his own son, Absalom, and chose to flee his throne in disgrace. In his miserable travels he confronted a resentful old ally of Saul's named Shimei. He threw stones at David, cursed him and called him a blood-thirsty scoundrel who was getting what he deserved.[27] Abishai, who was with David, promptly suggested he cut off Shimei's head.[28] You do not curse God's anointed! David's response reflects the lesson he learned from Abigail years before. David said that perhaps God had sent this man. At least, David said, God may "see my distress and repay me with good for the cursing."[29] David walked on in quiet dignity while rocks and dust continued to shower his head.[30] Later, when David returned to his throne, Shimei joined the welcoming throng of people. He fell humbly at David's feet. It was suggested he be executed, but David forgave him.[31] David had learned much about the Lord and was reflecting His glorious nature.[32] A king with compassion is marvelous. *Anyone* with compassion is a blessing.

DAVID, A MAN LIKE US ALL

David is an exceptional person to study. He was at various times a shepherd, court singer,[33] soldier and king. He could compose beautiful and inspired poem-songs[34] and he could also be a devastating warrior.[35] He was a passionate human being who allowed God to direct his heart. David experienced the highs and lows of life in dramatic ways.

---

[27] II Samuel 16:5-8

[28] II Samuel 16:9

[29] II Samuel 16:10-12

[30] II Samuel 16:13-14

[31] II Samuel 19:15-23

[32] Psalm 103:8-14; Romans 2:4; II Peter 3:9

[33] I Samuel 16:14-23; II Samuel 23:1

[34] II Samuel 1:17-27; 3:33-34; 22:1-51; 23:1-7; many of the Psalms

[35] I Samuel 18:6-7; 12-16; 30:1-30; II Samuel 5:17-25; 8:1-14

When the Philistines were finally subdued, the beloved ark of the covenant was at last returned to the tabernacle in Jerusalem. "David, wearing a linen ephod, danced before the Lord with all his might" while voices shouted and trumpets pealed.[36] When criticized for his indignity he stated he was ruler over the Lord's people Israel and he would celebrate before the Lord.[37] It was a glorious day for Israel and David knew how to rejoice. We too should know how to rejoice before the Lord.[38]

Years later David's son Absalom attempted to steal his throne. In the ensuing strife Absalom was killed in battle. Though David had been disgraced by Absalom and caused to flee like a dog, his constant inquiry was "Is the young man Absalom safe?"[39] When he learned of his death he wailed, "O my son Absalom! My son, my son Absalom! If only I had died instead of you -- O Absalom, my son, my son!"[40] The good king was willing to die for his wicked son. Again his Father's heart was showing. We should cultivate such an attitude.[41]

A DARK EVENT

Unfortunately when we speak of David, many think first about the immoral affair he had with Bathsheba, but this was only a tragic lapse in his life. David seemed to handle adversity well, perhaps because in the crises of his life he seemed always to inquire of the Lord what to do.[42] But during a moment of leisure, when his defenses were down, he looked... then stared... then inquired - not of the Lord, but about this woman, another man's wife. He slept with her and she became pregnant.[43] Then he compounded his sin

---

[36] II Samuel 6:14-15

[37] II Samuel 6:21

[38] Romans 12:12; Philippians 3:1; 4:4, 10

[39] II Samuel 18:5, 12, 29, 32

[40] II Samuel 18:33; 19:4

[41] John 15:13; Romans 5:6-8; I John 3:16

[42] I Samuel 23:2, 4, 9-14; 30:8; II Samuel 2:1; 5:19, 23

[43] II Samuel 11:1-5

with lying and by causing Bathsheba's husband Uriah to die in battle. A dark day in the life of an otherwise good king.

Nathan the prophet was dispatched and he told a story of a rich man who selfishly took his neighbor's only little pet lamb to kill for his friends. David was enraged! "You are the man," Nathan proclaimed.[44] David was deeply convicted and heartbroken. He pleaded for forgiveness and restoration to his old place with God[45] and God heard him and forgave him and restored him. The baby died. David grieved. He anticipated seeing the baby later on.[46]

DAVID'S LIFELONG DREAM: A TEMPLE

Perhaps above all else, David wanted to build a permanent structure for the ark of God; a temple instead of a tent.[47] Nathan the prophet gave his approval but was told by God that *David* was not to be allowed to build it. God would however establish David's family in the kingship and allow his son to build a temple.[48]

David must have been deeply disappointed, but he knew and trusted God. He went to his special prayer place. Forgetting the rejected request, he said, "who am I, Sovereign Lord, and what is my family, that You have brought me thus far?...Is this Your usual way of dealing with man, O Sovereign Lord?"[49] David was without adequate words to express his praise and thanks to the Lord. "How great You are, O Sovereign Lord! There is no one like You, and there is no God but You, as we have heard with our own ears."[50] "O Lord, our Lord, how majestic is Your name in all the earth" he wrote.[51] He never grew weary of praising God, writing page after page of the most uplifting songs of praise ever penned by man. "The

---

[44] II Samuel 12:1-7

[45] II Samuel 12:13-14; Psalm 32:1-5; Psalm 51

[46] II Samuel 12:14-23

[47] II Samuel 7:1-2

[48] II Samuel 7:3-17

[49] II Samuel 7:18-19

[50] II Samuel 7:20-24

[51] Psalm 8

Spirit of the Lord spoke through me; His word was on my tongue."[52] So David died as he lived, the great heart of God stirring and directing his daily walk.

We cannot significantly change our appearance, we cannot alter the world circumstances, but we can let our hearts become like God's. We can become a person after God's own heart, and we can live in joy.

---

[52]II Samuel 23:2

1. Why does God concentrate so heavily on the condition of one's heart?

2. What in David's heart and life made him able to confront and defeat Goliath?

3. What about the friendship between Jonathan and David demonstrates God's nature?

4. How did David's non-aggressive attitude toward his enemies serve him well in his later life? What are some ways we can imitate him?

5. Why was Abigail's advice to forgo his right to destroy Nabal a blessing in the life of David?

6. How can we develop the strength to act with the dignity David showed in regard to Shimei?

7. What was desirable about David's attitude toward Absalom? What was undesirable?

8. How could David survive such a tragic mistake as the Bathsheba-Uriah affair?

9. When did David turn in prayer and praise to God? Only in good times? Discuss examples.

There are some things you just don't do. On the lighter side, one man wrote: "you don't tug on Superman's cape; you don't spit into the wind; you don't pull the mask off the old Lone Ranger; and you don't mess around with Jim."[1] But there are some very serious "don't dos". Four that have been suggested are: You don't try to deceive God;[2] you don't demand that God prove Himself;[3] you don't accuse God of wrongdoing;[4] and you don't *ever* question what God does.

All these sound like compelling advice not to be ignored. But look again...at the last of these. Are we never to question the actions of God? It would seem so, but study the lives of God's honored followers and you will discover many of them did question God. Among them are Abraham, Moses, David, Job and Habakkuk. Let's examine carefully this difficult issue, for here we will open another facet of the fascinating depths of the nature of God.

GOOD FRIENDS SOMETIMES QUESTION EACH OTHER

Abraham had proven himself a faithful and obedient servant of God[5] and God lifted him to the position of friendship.[6] "Shall I hide from Abraham what I am about to do?"[7] Friends consult each other about mutually important matters.[8] God was about to destroy Sodom where Abraham's nephew Lot lived.[9] So God told Abraham. Abraham immediately began a straightforward discussion with God.

---

[1] Jim Croce, "You Don't Mess Around With Jim", 1971 song.

[2] Galatians 6:7; Numbers 32:23

[3] Deuteronomy 6:16; Matthew 4:7

[4] James 1:13; Psalm 119:138, 142

[5] Hebrews 11:8-10, 17-19; Genesis 18:17-19

[6] II Chronicles 20:7; Isaiah 41:8; James 2:23

[7] Genesis 18:17

[8] John 15:15

[9] Genesis 13:12-13; 14:12, 16

In fact, he questioned the proposed action of God. "Will you sweep away the righteous with the wicked? What if there are 50 righteous people in the city?...Far be it from You to do such a thing -- to kill the righteous with the wicked, treating the righteous and the wicked alike. Far be it from You! Will not the Judge of all the earth do right?"[10]

We might have expected lightening to strike or an earthquake to begin. Abraham had stood up and questioned the proposed action of God. He almost challenged God to live up to His reputation as the righteous Judge of the universe. Would God roar like an angry lion?[11] God's response is most educational. No fire, no anger. He simply took up the discussion with Abraham[12] Together they sort of bartered over how many righteous people had to be in Sodom to save it -- 50? 45? 40? 30? 20? or even 10. God agreed to each new less-demanding requirement. The two friends agreed. Abraham questioned God, but do we dare do this?

If God is your friend, then you can. But do it like Abraham. First, make sure you are presenting a request consistent with the righteous nature of God. Remember, God cannot ignore sin; it must be dealt with.[13] Then always approach God with humility and reverence.[14] "Now that I have been so bold as to speak to the Lord, though I am but dust and ashes... may the Lord not be angry, but let me speak just once more."[15] Finally, be willing to accept what the Lord decides. When ten righteous people were not uncovered in Sodom, it was destroyed. Lot and his family could flee, but Sodom had to go. Abraham apparently said no more.[16] God was acting as the righteous Judge of the earth and Abraham accepted God's role, but God also recognized Abraham's distress and patiently answered his misunderstandings. God wants us too, to know and understand

---

[10]Genesis 18:23-25

[11]Amos 3:8

[12]Genesis 18:23-33

[13]Exodus 34:7; Nahum 1:3; Romans 3:21-26

[14]Psalm 95:6

[15]Genesis 18:27; 32

[16]Genesis 19:1-26

Him.[17] If this requires questions and clarification, He seems most willing to help us.

HUMBLE MOSES QUESTIONED GOD OFTEN

It appears that God and Moses in their joint enterprise to bring Israel to the promised land often had very lively face to face conversations.[18] It all seemed to begin when Moses became bogged down with the burden of leading all those people.[19] God knew that it was overwhelming for Moses and He allowed Moses to state his feelings, frustrations and perceived needs in a strikingly open way. Two noteworthy examples are valuable to examine.[20]

The people's constant complaining about food had beaten Moses to a near pulp. Finally Moses slumped into the familiar meeting place[21] and poured out his frustrated heart. The questions gushed out "Why have You brought this trouble on Your servant? What have I done to displease You that You put the burden of all the people on me? Did I conceive all the people? Did I give them birth? Why do You tell me to carry them in my arms, as a nurse carries an infant?...Where can I get meat for all these people?... If this is how You are going to treat me, put me to death right now.."[22]

Strong words and hard questions, and all directed at God, but God understood. He felt compassion for His servant and friend Moses. No rebuke was forthcoming. Only a solution to the problem: a little decentralization of decision making, some relief from the burden, God's Spirit spread around, and others assisting Moses.[23] Even when Moses questioned further whether the food problem had been resolved, God simply but pointedly responded, "Is the Lord's arm

---

[17]Jeremiah 9:24
[18]Exodus 33:7-13
[19]Exodus 32:7-14; 33:12-23
[20]Numbers 11:10-17, 18-23; 14:10-25
[21]Exodus 29:42-45; 33:7-11
[22]Numbers 11:11-15
[23]Numbers 11:16-20

too short? You will now see whether or not what I say will now come true for you."[24]

A little later the people of Israel again rebelled against God and threatened to stone Moses.[25] God suggested that He strike them all down with a plague and start a new nation from the family of Moses.[26] Moses sternly rejected this idea and questioned God's proposal. "If You put these people to death all at one time, the nations..will say, 'the Lord was not able to bring these people into the land He promised them on earth..."[27] Moses goes on saying, "Now may the Lord's strength be displayed, just as you have declared; 'The Lord is slow to anger, abounding in love and forgiving sin and rebellion. Yet he does not leave the guilty unpunished; He punishes the children for the sin of the fathers to the third and fourth generations.' In accordance with Your great love, forgive the sin of these people, just as You have pardoned them from the time they left Egypt until now."[28] In response to Moses' lecture, God replied, "I have forgiven them."[29] But He went on to announce that none of the rebellious people would ever reach the promised land.[30] Moses accepted God's decision. When one is wholeheartedly doing God's will and encounters difficulties, these should openly be addressed to God. He can handle complaints, expressions of frustration, even openly rash statements. We must never forget that He is the Lord, but He will never forget that you are weak as dust,[31] and He will treat you as a friend. Always.

---

[24]Numbers   11:21-23
[25]Numbers   14:1-10
[26]Numbers   14:10-12; Exodus   32:7-14
[27]Numbers   14:13-16
[28]Numbers   14:17-19; Exodus   34:6-7; 20:5-6; Psalm   78:38
[29]Numbers   14:20
[30]Numbers   14:21-35
[31]Psalm   103:13-18

The book of Job contains an extensive analysis of God by the four friends of Job[32] and by Job himself. It rolls on for chapter after chapter.[33] In his despair, Job expresses many tough questions: "Why did I not perish at birth...why is light given to those in misery and life to the bitter in soul?"[34] Remember, O God, that my life is but a breath... why do You not pardon my offenses..?"[35] "I will say to God: Do not condemn me, but tell me what charges You have against me."[36] "As surely as God lives, who has denied me justice.."[37] "Oh that I had someone to hear me!... let the Almighty answer me."[38] And then the Lord God did answer him.[39]

God identifies all this discussion and questioning as that which "darkens My counsel" and as that which was without knowledge. He then refused to answer the charges against Him and the many distortions of His nature expressed by Job and the four. He simply affirmed His tremendous superiority over all this drivel. He is, after all, the Almighty God. "Will the one who contends with the Almighty correct Him?"[40] Job was overwhelmed. "I am unworthy - how can I reply to You? I put my hand over my mouth. I spoke once; I have no answer - twice, but I will say no more."[41]

God continued. "Brace yourself like a man; I will question you, and you shall answer Me. Would you discredit my justice? Would you condemn Me to justify yourself? Do you have an arm like God's and can you make your voice thunder like His?"[42] God clearly

---

[32]Eliphaz, Bildad, Zophar and Elihu; Job 2:11; 32:1-2

[33]Job   3-37

[34]Job   3:11,20

[35]Job   7:7,21

[36]Job   10:2

[37]Job   27:2

[38]Job   31:35

[39]Job   38-42

[40]Job   40:1-2

[41]Job   40:3-5

[42]Job   40:6-9

established for Job who was who and Job humbly assumed his rightful place,[43] but God did not punish Job for his questioning during his duress. Nor did God lower the high opinion He held of Job.[44] He blessed him more abundantly than ever before.[45]

There seems to be no penalty for questioning God; if you have made Him your Lord and friend, you can ask, you can express your doubts, frustrations and complaints. His shoulders are infinitely broad. His understanding is limitless. He loves you and will give you answers, comfort, instruction, or whatever you need, and all without any put-down.[46] He is not intimidated by our questions.

When Habakkuk vigorously complained that God was using a more wicked people (Assyria) to punish a less wicked people (Israel),[47] God gave him straight-forward answers.[48] Habakkuk then poured forth majestic praise. "I stand in awe of Your deeds, O Lord... I will be joyful in God my Savior. The Sovereign Lord is my strength; He makes my feet like the feet of a deer, He enables me to go on the heights."[49] If we approach God as our Sovereign Lord and our beloved friend, we will find our bitter complaints and burdensome questions ultimately turned to praise.

The Israelites complained that it was of no value to live right and serve God. Evil men prosper and they get away with it.[50] God told the Israelites that they were saying harsh things about Him,[51] yet He then answered enthusiastically that "they will be Mine... in the day when I make up my treasured possession... you will again see the distinction... between those who serve God and those who do

---

43 Job   42:1-6
44 Job   1:6-8; 2:3-6
45 Job   42:7-17
46 James   1:5-6
47 Habakkuk   1:1-4,12-17
48 Habakkuk   1:5-11; 2:1-20
49 Habakkuk   3:2,18-19
50 Malachi   3:14-15
51 Malachi 3:13

not..."[52] It is worth it to serve God. He will make it all right. He always does.

Of course there are others in the Bible who questioned God, including David[53] and Jeremiah.[54] Questioning God does not show disrespect for Him, but rather recognizes that He is the Sovereign Lord. It says we are looking to Him for answers, looking to Him to bring justice and mercy to pass.

It is alright to talk to God... and to question God, but to go on disputing God's decisions and questioning His actions after He has responded is dangerous. God is never unjust, and to insist that He is, is spiritual self-destruction.

"Then why does God still blame us? For who resists His will? But who are you, O man, to talk back to God? Shall what is formed say to Him who formed it, 'why did you make me like this'?"[55]

What a God we serve! He wants us informed. He wants us to feel comfort in our distress.[56] He wants us to bare our hearts to Him.

The more you learn about God, the more enamored you will be of Him. He is an approachable Father and friend. How easy it is to love Him. And to serve Him.

---

[52]Malachi 3:16-4:4

[53]II Samuel 6:8 (he thought it, if he did not express it.)

[54]Jeremiah   12:1-13;20:7-18

[55]Romans 9:19-21ff

[56]II Corinthians 1:3-7

1. Why might we think that God is never to be questioned?

2. Who are some Biblical characters who questioned God?

3. Why do you think God chose to sort of negotiate the matter of Sodom's destruction with Abraham?

4. Contrast the way Abraham questioned God with what you believe would be wrong ways to question God.

5. How did God deal with Moses' pointed, and often bitter, questions?

6. What qualities in your life need to be in a state of cultivation if you are going to question God?

7. What response did God give to Job and his friends after they had discussed His nature and Job had questioned His actions?

8. What did God say to the charge that the wicked prosper while the righteous gain nothing for doing right?

9. Discuss the difference between questioning God and "talking back to God" (Romans 9:19-21)

Old Samuel felt rejected when the people desired to push aside his priestly leadership in favor of a king like the other nations had.[1] But God informed Samuel it was really God who was being rejected. He was all the King they needed.[2]

We humans have always seemed to have difficulties with spiritual leadership. We seek more tangible leaders. We would rather push Jesus Christ onto an earthly throne than allow Him to reign in our hearts.[3] We would keep God at a distance as merely our King, lawgiver, ruler and judge. He is all of these, but He desires to be much more. He wants to be much closer and more involved with us; to walk with us as He did with Enoch.[4] While we would sit stewing in our own difficulties and guilt, God calls us to meet face to face with Him as He did with Moses[5] and reason things out like He did with Abraham.[6] "Draw near to Me," He implores over and over.[7] But we pull back and hide amid the trees of our guilt.[8] We allow our sin to separate between us and God.[9]

WE SPEAK OF ORGANIZATION; GOD SPEAKS OF RELATIONSHIPS

Often we express the same attitude today as ancient Israel did in seeking a king. We often speak of the church as an institution or an organization. God never used such expressions. To Him the church

---

[1] I Samuel 8:1-6

[2] I Samuel 8:7-8

[3] John 6:15; 18:36

[4] Genesis 3:8; 5:24; Leviticus 26:12; Deuteronomy 10:12-13; Micah 6:8; II Corinthians 6:16

[5] Exodus 33:7,11; Isaiah 41:1; Hebrews 4:14-16

[6] Genesis 18:17-33; Isaiah 1:18

[7] Hebrews 7:19; 10:22; James 4:8; II Chronicles 15:1-2

[8] Genesis 3:8-10

[9] Isaiah 59:1-2

is the very body of Christ.[10] We are the family of God[11] and we are over and over again affectionately referred to as the sons and daughters of God.[12] Jesus came to bring "many sons to glory"[13] not many subjects into the organization. He is most emphatic on this point. "So you are no longer a slave, but a son; and since you are a son, God also made you an heir."[14] We speak of leadership for the church while the Spirit of God speaks of shepherdship.[15] Feeding and caring tenderly for His sheep is God's goal,[16] not efficiently directing the church like a board of directors.

In human organizations, corporate executive and appointed directors hand out directives and everyone is to comply or else depart. The family of God was never to be anything like this. With God you lead by serving. It's not what others are going to do for you but what can you do for them. Leadership in God's family is done from the serving end of the table.[17] Everything is to be done with a family orientation, not a worldly business approach. This does not mean it is wrong to be organized. Families need to be organized, but not like an efficient business or an army. Among the people of God, love, sacrifice and giving prevail. It is relationships.

OUR FATHER, THE GOD OF RELATIONSHIPS

Since God is a person, He cannot rightly be called an "it". It was decided to refer to Him as a "He" but this does not mean He does not possess the characteristics we usually describe as feminine. In fact, He is described as exhibiting the finest characteristics of a mother and even more so than human mothers. He comforts like a

---

[10]I Corinthians 12:12-27; Ephesians 1:23

[11]Ephesians 3:15; Hebrews 2:11-13

[12]Matthew 5:9; Luke 20:36; John 11:52; John 1:12-13; Romans 8:14-17,21; 9:8,26; Galatians 3:26, 4:1-7; I John 3:1-3, 5:2 and many others

[13]Hebrews 2:9-10

[14]Galatians 4:7

[15]I Peter 5:1-4

[16]Jeremiah 23:1-8; Ezekiel 34:1-24; John 21:15-16; Acts 20:28

[17]Matthew 20:24-28; 23:8-12; Luke 22:24-27; John 13:1-17

mother does a child.[18] While an earthly mother might abandon the infant at her breast (our newspapers have painfully borne this out), God says He could never do this. "See, I have engraved you on the palms of My hands"[19] He announced to His people. Like the noble wife-mother of Proverbs 31, He is the One who notices the poor and needy and reaches out to help them.[20] Our God has all the compassion and sensitivity which we see reflected in the women He created.[21] He is not only our spiritual Father, He is our spiritual mother as well.

He is also our beloved friend. Not just the friend of Abraham or Moses, [22]but the friend of all who submit to His will and seek to obey all His commandments. When we love each other as He has loved us, He no longer calls us servants who know nothing but rather friends who can know all.[23] He loves us like both a mother and a father and He treats us like friends. His goal is nothing less than deep fellowship with us.[24] In fact, one of His favorite illustrations of His feeling for us and His desire for us is the husband-wife relationship.[25] Let's look at this.

YOUR MAKER IS YOUR HUSBAND

God opens His appeal to Israel through Isaiah with the tragic announcement that He had reared children and brought them up but they had rebelled. His own people did not know and understand Him.[26] They sought a God kept at a safe distance. Going through the worship forms, but never really drawing near to God.[27] Keep-

---

[18]Isaiah 66:13

[19]Isaiah 49:13-16

[20]Proverbs 31:20; Psalms 10:14; Deuteronomy 10:18

[21]Genesis 2:21-22

[22]James 2:23, Exodus 33:11

[23]John 15:15-17

[24]I John 1:3; I Corinthians 1:9

[25]Ephesians 5:21-33; Romans 7:1-6

[26]Isaiah 1:2-3

[27]Isaiah 1:10-17; 29:13; Matthew 15:3-9

ing the feasts and the prayer times, but neglecting to care for people in need.[28] In other words, they ignored relationships.

But walking with God *is* relationship. It's first of all loving God with all that is in you,[29] and then inseparably we are to love our neighbors and do good to them.[30] Out of this love and these relationships emerge all that exists between God and mankind. We obey Him because of this loving relationship.[31] We do not become His children *because* we do good works. We do good works because He has made us His own.[32]

So He makes His throbbing appeal to His perishing people. "Your Maker is your husband - the Lord almighty is His name...you were a wife deserted...for a brief moment I abandoned you, but with deep compassion I will bring you back. In a surge of anger I hid My face from you for a moment, but with everlasting kindness I will have compassion on you."[33] He goes on to promise that His unfailing love will never be shaken.[34] He longs to again rejoice over them like a bridegroom does over his bride.[35] You broke my covenant even "though I was a husband to you.[36] Return, faithless people...for I am your husband."[37] You can always return to your Maker.

Hosea relates for us a stirring account. In this story Hosea is wed to Gomer. They have three children.[38] But Gomer is an unfaithful, immoral prodigal. He painfully describes her adulteries in graphic

---

[28]Isaiah 1:15-17; Amos 5:18-24; Isaiah 58:3-11
[29]Deuteronomy 6:4-6; Matthew 22:36-38
[30]Leviticus 19:18; Matthew 22:39-40; Luke 10:25-37
[31]Deuteronomy 6:1-6; John 14:15
[32]Ephesians 2:8-10
[33]Isaiah 54:5-8
[34]Isaiah 54:10
[35]Isaiah 62:4-5; 65:19
[36]Jeremiah 31:32
[37]Jeremiah 3:14
[38]Hosea 1:2-11

detail.[39] She even credits her assorted lovers with providing her with the material goods which actually came from her husband.[40] Brokenhearted, he charts his plans. He will cut her off from her lovers so she will discover he is the one who has lovingly provided for her needs.[41] Then despite her atrocious behavior, he will court her anew. He will allure her into a lonely place and speak tenderly to her. He will restore her to her former lofty position. "In that day you will call me 'my husband'; you will no longer call me 'my master'."[42] He will restore her to intimacy and bless her life despite her past cruelties.[43]

But she does not come back. She plunges deeper and deeper in degradation. Apparently her lovers grow tired of her. She has grown haggard and unattractive. She is in shambles. Finally, she is led to the trading block to be sold as a slave. And standing in the auction crowd is her brokenhearted husband. He is disgraced but his love is greater than his shame. The bidding begins. It is low. After all, what's a worn out prostitute worth? A quivering voice is heard in the crowd. "I'll pay 15 shekels of silver and 10 bushels of barley for her." "Sold!" shouts the auctioneer.[44]

Gomer looks at her new owner. It is Hosea. He has bought his own wife, the unfaithful and defiled wife of his youth. His love will not die. Against all common sense, he gives her yet another chance. "You are to live with me many days; you must not be a prostitute or be intimate with any man, and I will live with you."[45]

But the story is really about God and His people.[46] God is the unrelenting lover who just won't give up. His love knows no quit-

---

[39] Hosea 2:2-5

[40] Hosea 2:5

[41] Hosea 2:6-13

[42] Hosea 2:14-16

[43] Hosea 2:16-23

[44] Hosea 3:1-2, along with supposed details not included in the text.

[45] Hosea 3:3

[46] Hosea 2:5

ting place, yet He cannot live with her in her adulteries.[47] We too must turn away from our sin, but He always wants us back. No matter what, we must not underestimate the love and willingness to forgive which our Father possesses. It is for you. It is for your brother, your neighbor, and even your enemies.[48]

HOW BIG IS THE HEART OF GOD?

Hosea goes on. Chapter after chapter outlines God's case against sinful Israel. His chosen and beloved and rebellious people. "There is no faithfulness, no love, no knowledge of God in the land."[49] In other words, no relationship between God and His people. This is the ultimate problem - now as well as then. In chapter 11 the book of Hosea reaches a climax. God has chronicled Israel's multiplied sins;[50] now He expresses His deep hurt. Broken relationships hurt... deeply. "When Israel was a child, I loved him...taught Ephraim to walk, taking him by the arms..led them with cords of human kindness, with ties of love...bent down to feed them."[51] But Israel had rebelled so excessively; their sin was so grievous, it was time "to put an end to their plans."[52] He decides it should be cut-off time so that "even if they call on the Most High, He will by no means exalt them."[53]

But then His great heart is overwhelmed. "How can I give you up, Ephraim? How can I hand you over, Israel?...My heart is changed within Me; all my compassion is aroused. I will not carry out my fierce anger, nor will I turn and devastate Ephraim...for I am God, and not man -- the Holy One among you. I will not come in wrath."[54]

---

[47] Hosea 2:2

[48] I John 2:2

[49] Hosea 4:1

[50] Hosea chapters 4-10

[51] Hosea 11:1-4

[52] Hosea 11:6

[53] Hosea 11:7

[54] Hosea 11:8-9

Our sin deeply grieves our Father. It is an awesome and awful thing to dare displease and grieve our great Father. If we remain in sin, we will perish.[55] But if our hearts are turned, if we weary of our sin and it breaks our hearts,[56] if we turn to our Father, He will receive us. No matter where we have been. No matter how low.

Where is the dwelling place of God? Some would sequester Him in a temple or a church building. Impossible.[57] The whole earth will not contain Him. But there is a special dwelling place where God longs to be. He will go there whenever invited and stay there as long as He is treated as an honored guest and made welcome. "For this is what the high and lofty One says - He who lives forever, whose name is holy: I live in a high and holy place, but also with him who is contrite and lowly in spirit, to revive the spirit of the lowly and to revive the heart of the contrite."[58] He wants to be your God and walk with you, but He wants to move closer. He wants to make His dwelling place with you.[59] "Jesus replied, 'If anyone loves Me, he will obey my teaching. My Father will love him, and we will come to him and make our home with him'."[60]

"What is man that you are mindful of man, the son of man that you care for him?"[61] Can this be? God wants to live in me. In me! What kind of God is this? A kind One. A Holy One. And He wants you. And me. To live with us. Forever. Awesome!

---

[55]John 8:24; Romans 6:23; Luke 13:3-5

[56]Isaiah 66:2; Psalm 32:1-5; 51:15-17

[57]I Kings 8:27; Acts 17:24

[58]Isaiah 57:15

[59]Leviticus 26:12; Ezekiel 37:27; II Corinthians 6:16

[60]John 14:23

[61]Psalm 8:4

1. When Israel demanded a king, what were they really saying to God?

2. In what ways do we try to push God away and keep Him at a distance?

3. Can the church be successfully run by business principles? Discuss.

4. In what ways is God like a mother to us?

5. How important is relationship in God's dealing with us? Discuss.

6. "Your Maker is your husband" God said. Discuss the significance of this.

7. Discuss the purpose of the Gomer/Hosea story as it relates to us as God's people today.

8. How big is the heart of God? Illustrate.

9. What preparations and ongoing "upkeep" should we exercise in making ourselves acceptable dwelling places for God?

"Thou hast conquered, O pale Galilean; the world has grown gray from thy breath."[1] Certainly not a complimentary view of Jesus, nor of His Father whose nature He perfectly reflects.[2] Many others as well have considered God as a bit of a killjoy; He may be powerful, but He's not really much for fun, or laughter, or excitement. Or is He?

When He emblazoned our vast universe with stars, He knew we would look up in wonderment.[3] He knew we would try to count the stars and fail.[4] He knew we would invent powerful telescopes and discover new, far-flung galaxies containing more billions of stars. He knew we would measure and figure and reach the astounding conclusion that the closest star would take years to reach even in a vessel traveling at the incredible speed of light.[5]

He also knew we would fashion microscopes which would reveal that even a tiny drop of pond water is teeming with thousands of one-celled creatures. Complex little creatures. He knew we would explore our jungles and rivers and mountains and find such a variety of insects, animals and plants that they virtually defy thorough classification. We would find such colors, textures, aromas and sounds as to challenge our senses beyond their ability to comprehend.

Can you not imagine a sparkle in His eye as He watches us make amazing discovery after discovery. How could a dull God make such a dazzling and spectacular world? Evidently God takes pleasure

---

[1] Charles Swinburne
[2] Hebrews 1:1-3; John 1:18; 14:9
[3] Isaiah 40:25-26; Psalm 8:3
[4] Genesis 15:5
[5] About 186,276 miles per second

in a sweet smell or delightful sight.[6] And He made it all for us to relish.[7]

When He had His people construct a tabernacle, it was colorful, ornate and symmetrical.[8] The garments of the priests were lively colored.[9] Our Father is not the author of drabness or dullness. The world will never grow gray beneath His creative breath.[10]

THE FATHER OF PLEASURE AND REJOICING

God's world was deliberately composed for the beneficial use of mankind.[11] It was good. Very good.[12] Eden's garden overflowed with things pleasing to the eye and palate.[13] Since it was made to be enjoyed, then enjoying it brought glory to the Creator. The same is true today.

Using our freedom given us in Christ to indulge our sinful natures and thus re-enslave ourselves is forbidden.[14] The pleasures of sin are always for a short time and then payments come due.[15] Broken homes, devastated lives and death are the dividends sin distributes. But God intended us to cherish each day as a gift from His hand.[16] Life with Him is abundant life.[17] To live in an indifferent and half-hearted way is an insult to the Lord.[18]

---

[6] Genesis 8:20-21

[7] Genesis 1:26-31; 2:8-9; Psalm 104:14-15

[8] Exodus chapters 25-28

[9] Exodus 39:1-31

[10] Genesis 2:7; Psalm 104:29-30 (the word for breath and spirit are the same in Hebrew)

[11] Genesis 1:26-31

[12] Genesis 1:10,12,18,21,25,31; Psalm 104:24; I Timothy 4:4

[13] Genesis 2:9

[14] Galatians 5:1,13,19-21

[15] Romans 2:8-9; 6:23; Colossians 3:25

[16] Psalm 118:24

[17] John 10:10

[18] Revelation 3:15-16; Romans 12:11; Colossians 3:23-24

Married love and the unique sexual pleasures reserved for this relationship are unblushingly presented in the scriptures.[19] It was mankind in their guilt who cast embarrassed shadows over this beautiful gift of God. Victorian hypocrisy should not be blamed on God.

Rejoicing is stamped deeply on the nature of God. He made us to rejoice. Literally hundreds of Bible passages present this theme. When He gave His written law code on Mt. Sinai, He included three feasts which were to be celebrated each year.[20] They were not to simply offer yearly compliance to these events; they were to vigorously celebrate them. "And rejoice before the Lord...you, your sons and daughters...for the Lord your God will bless you in all your harvest and in all the work of your hands, and your joy will be complete."[21]

After years of captivity and disappointment the freed Israelites gathered to celebrate the freshly rebuilt Jerusalem walls. As the Book of the Law was being read and explained, the people began to weep. But Nehemiah intervened. It was time to eat and celebrate.[22] Abundant food and great joy carried the day. And soon the reading led them to the feasts. Especially the feast of tabernacles.[23] So for seven days they stopped everything and celebrated this feast. It hadn't been this good for hundreds of years. Their joy was very great.[24] Ours will be also when we begin to understand better the God we serve. He loves celebration. When these same people later held a massive celebration, complete with two large choirs, the rejoicing was splendid.[25] They were "rejoicing because God had given them great joy. The women and children also rejoiced. The

---

[19]Genesis 18:12; 26:8; Deuteronomy 24:5; Song of Solomon (entire); Proverbs 5:18-19; I Corinthians 7:1-7
[20]Exodus 23:14-17; Deuteronomy 16:1-17
[21]Deuteronomy 16:11;13-15
[22]Nehemiah 8:1-12
[23]Either Leviticus 23:33-43; Numbers 29:12-40 or Deuteronomy 16:13-17
[24]Nehemiah 8:13-18
[25]Nehemiah 12:27-47

sound of rejoicing in Jerusalem could be heard far away."[26] And the One who treasured this jubilation the most was the Father above who was being honored. We can honor God in no higher way then to celebrate Him with all our being.[27] All their worship was to be a celebration. Their burnt offerings, sacrifices and tithing days were times to greatly rejoice "because the Lord your God has blessed you."[28] "But may the righteous be glad and rejoice before God; may they be happy and joyful."[29] We should always come into God's presence full of thanksgiving and ready to celebrate His goodness.[30]

A CROWN OF BEAUTY INSTEAD OF ASHES

What is the source of all artistic creativity? It is from the God who created us and who is all in all.[31] The yearning to paint or form a sculpture are imitations of our Creator-Father. "Is anyone happy? Let him sing songs of praise."[32] Does not God call out of our hearts songs of joy?[33] "Sing to God, sing praise to His name; extol Him who rides on the clouds - His name is the Lord - rejoice before Him."[34]

And what about dancing. A noted preacher once said, "a dancing foot and a praying knee cannot grow on the same leg." I respectfully submit that he was mistaken. David prayed often[35] but also danced with all his might before the Lord.[36] And his critic, not David, was

---

[26]Nehemiah 12:43

[27]Luke 1:13-14

[28]Deuteronomy 12:4-7

[29]Psalm 68:3

[30]Psalm 33:21; Psalm 34:1-3; 35:9; Ephesians 5:19-20 and many others

[31]John 1:3; Ephesians 1:23; Colossians 1:15-16; 3:11; Hebrews 1:2-3

[32]James 5:13

[33]Psalm 65:8; Psalm 100

[34]Psalm 68:4

[35]I Samuel 23:2,4,10-12; 30:8; II Samuel 2:1; 5:19; 7:18-29

[36]II Samuel 6:14-19

cursed by the Lord.[37] Dancing is a natural form of celebration.[38] In Bible times it often was practiced to express happiness and joy.[39]It was encouraged by God as a way to praise Him.[40] It was one way to show that God had turned ones sorrow into joy.[41] God is good at doing this if we give Him opportunity. When the prodigal son came home in Jesus' beautiful story, the celebration included music and dancing.[42] There is indeed "a time to mourn and a time to dance".[43] This does not endorse the erotic dancing of Salome[44] nor any other debased form of dancing. Degrading art, whether painting, sculpture, music or dancing is like any distortion of God's gifts - sinful; but practiced as God intended, these all glorify the Creator.

God is incredibly poetic. He inspired a majority of the writers of the Bible to utilize poetry. Of the 39 Old Testament books, 34 contain poetry.[45] Most of the writings from Job to Malachi are in Hebrew poetic form, and 18 New Testament letters contain some poetry. Some writings are believed to be parts of songs.[46] Even God's people are referred to as the "poetry of God"[47] and God will be our ode to life when we see Him as He really is.

A WORD ABOUT OUR FATHER AND MONEY

The Bible never says money is evil. Loving money spawns all kinds of trouble.[48] People are to be loved; money is to serve human

---

[37]II Samuel 6:20-23
[38]Luke 6:23; Acts 3:8
[39]I Samuel 18:6-7; 21:11; 29:5; Exodus 15:20-21
[40]Psalm 149:3; 150:4
[41]Psalm   30:11-12
[42]Luke   15:23-25
[43]Ecclesiastes 3:4
[44]Matthew 14:6-7
[45]All but Leviticus, Ruth, Nehemiah, Esther, and Haggai
[46]Phillippians 2:6-11; I Timothy 6:16; II Timothy 2:11-13
[47]Ephesians 2:10 - "workmanship" is "poema" in Greek
[48]I   Timothy   6:6-10,17-19

needs. God gives us the ability to earn wealth.[49] Abraham was wealthy and knew that it all came from the Lord. So, like God, he was generous.[50] Job was highly prosperous.[51] During his time of extreme affliction, he expressed his sharing attitude to his friends.[52] At the end, he received even more.[53]

God loves to give gifts to us, gracious and abundant gifts.[54] God desires for us to make money so we can share it with others.[55] An openhanded sharing with the poor and needy reflects the nature of God and shows our trust that He will provide for us.[56] "The righteous give generously"[57] and God promises to bless their generosity.[58] We give to God not because He needs our gifts[59] but so we can reflect His beautiful nature through our lives.[60] It is a deadly and fearsome thing to receive from God and not share with those in need.[61]

SHOULD WE ALWAYS BE "SENSIBLE"?

What does God think when we, out of spontaneous love, buy something a bit "foolish" for our mate? Or a friend? Jesus addressed this issue dramatically, because a woman named Mary did this very thing. She loved Jesus and poured on Him some very expensive

---

[49]Deuteronomy 8:17-18; Proverbs 10:22
[50]Genesis 13:5-9; 14:18-23; 18:3-8; 24:34-35
[51]Job 1:1-3
[52]Job 31:16-25
[53]Job 42:12-17
[54]Malachi 3:10; James 1:17
[55]Ephesians 4:28; Luke 3:11
[56]Deuteronomy 14:28-29; 15:7-11; II Corinthians 9:6-15
[57]Psalm 37:21
[58]Psalm 112:1-9
[59]Psalm 50:7-10
[60]Psalm 68:5-6; Proverbs 14:31
[61]Proverbs 14:31; 17:5; 21:13; Luke 16:19-31; I John 3:16-17

oil.[62] Actually, this happened more than once.[63] Why did Jesus seem so approachable? Because He was not the "pale Galilean" but rather the one who joyfully ate and drank with people. So much so that some falsely called Him a glutton and drunkard.[64] He understood the embarrassment of a father who had run out of wine at a wedding feast and He eliminated his potential disgrace.[65]

After Mary had poured out her impulsive and costly gift on Jesus, the critics moved in. "Such waste! What about the poor and needy?" Jesus silenced them all and warmly endorsed her courageous action.[66] We should constantly be serving the poor. Jesus exhibited this above all others;[67] and there are times to openly, even lavishly, show our love to others.

OUR FATHER AND HIS SON ARE EXCITING

What a God we serve... and His Son is just like Him. He came to bring His people joy and His joy is made complete when we learn to rejoice.[68] "The kingdom of God is not a matter of eating and drinking, but of righteousness, peace and joy in the Holy Spirit, because anyone who serves Christ in this way is pleasing to God and approved by men."[69] When we attune our lives with His, He takes delight in us and "as a bridegroom rejoices over his bride, so will your God rejoice over you."[70]

Our Father is alive and He is the source of life and of all that is good. He longs now to bring each of us home to Him - to live with Him now in warm fellowship,[71] and to live with Him forever in

---

[62]Matthew 26:6-13; Mark 14:1-9; John 12:1-8
[63]Luke 7:36-50
[64]Matthew 11:19; 9:11-13; Luke 5:29-35
[65]John 2:1-11
[66]Matthew 26:10-13; Luke 7:44-50
[67]Luke 4:17-21; John 12:8; 13:29
[68]John 15:11; 16:20-24; 17:13
[69]Romans 14:17-18; Luke 2:52
[70]Isaiah 62:4-5
[71]John 14:23; II Corinthians 6:16-18; I John 1:3-4

heaven.[72] And did you know that God can sing? Your homecoming will be so overwhelming that all heaven will break out in rejoicing[73] and God Himself will sing in joy over you:

"The Lord your God is with you,
He is mighty to save.
He will take great delight in you,
He will quiet you with His love,
He will rejoice over you with singing."[74]

[72]John 14:1-3; I Thessalonians 4:17
[73]Luke 15:7,10
[74]Zephaniah 3:17

1. What does the spectacular size, variety and beauty of the universe tell us about our Father?

2. How would you describe our Father's view of pleasure?

3. What did ancient Israel do in their God-appointed celebrations? What attitude were they to maintain?

4. What kind of celebrations should we engage in today in order to bring glory to our Father?

5. In Isaiah 61:3, God promises to bestow "a crown of beauty instead of ashes". What are some ways He does this today?

6. What are some correct uses of music and dancing and some wrong uses of them?

7. What does the large amount of poetry adorning the scriptures suggest to us about the nature of our Father?

8. What does sharing generously with the poor and resourceless have to do with the nature of God?

9. While we should live moderately and share our resources with the needy, is there a place for occasional "foolish" spending? Discuss

10. Can God sing? If so, what is it that stirs the Father's great heart and causes Him to burst forth in joyful singing?

81

Notes

God sent out His birth announcements early... about 1,000 years early. "I will be his Father, and he will be My Son."[1] Even earlier He had made allusions to His coming[2] and many other previews were to be given later in Isaiah[3] and other places.[4]

We have all discussed what we call the preexistence of Christ. Obviously Jesus was with the Father even before the foundations of our world were laid.[5] But on a remarkable day in history, Jesus left the glory of the heavenly existence and became the developing infant of a peasant woman named Mary.[6] All of time had reached its center point. Time became divided into B.C. and A.D. and rightly so.

OUR GOD BECOMES A FATHER

Jesus Christ was the Son of man.[7] This is how He normally addressed Himself.[8] He developed nine months in Mary's womb like other babies.[9] He was born,[10] consecrated[11] and raised[12] in the

---

[1]II Samuel 7:14; Psalm 89:26-29; Hebrews 1:5

[2]Genesis 3:15 - (Romans 16:20); Deuteronomy 18:15, 18-19

[3]Isaiah 7:14; 9:6-7; 11:1-10; 42:1-4; 52:13-53:12; 61:1-3

[4]Micah 5:2; Daniel 7:13-14

[5]John 1:1-4, 14,17: 8:56-58: 17:5,24; Ephesians 1:4; Colossians 1:15-20; Hebrews 1:1-3; I Peter 1:20; Revelation 13:8

[6]Phillippians 2:5-8; Galatians 4:4; Matthew 1:18-25; Luke 1:26-38

[7]He is called this about 65 times in the Gospels.

[8]Matthew 8:20; 16:13; Luke 19:10; John 5:27 and many others

[9]Luke 1:36,39-45,56; 2:1-7

[10]Luke 2:4-12

[11]Luke 2:22-24; Leviticus 12:8 - the offering of the poor was given

[12]Luke 2:39-40; John 1:45-46

humblest of human conditions. He was made just like His human brothers and sisters.[13] He felt pain, disappointment and happiness just like we do. He was tempted like we are. He can be touched by our weaknesses because He was just like us,[14] a dust man.[15] He was no distant deity off in the clouds... He was "God with us",[16] yet He was also God "one of us".

While Jesus Christ was the Son of man, He was also the Son of God. He was conceived in the womb of Mary by the Holy Spirit of God.[17] Many thought Him to be the son of Joseph the carpenter,[18] but He was truly the Son of God. "You are my Son, today I have become your Father."[19] When He was born, a simple but profound celebration took place. Angels, shepherds and mysterious wisemen celebrated, along with Mary and Joseph.[20] The baby grew up in lowly Nazareth.[21] At age 12 he lingered in Jerusalem after the Passover Feast. He asked his worried parents, "didn't you know I had to be in my Father's house?"[22]...My Father's house.

Soon Jesus was 30 years old.[23] He knew His Father wanted Him to go to the one who had been preparing the way for Him,[24] so He sought and received the baptism of John. He did this to please His Father.[25] His Father sent the Holy Spirit in dove form to rest on

---

[13] Hebrews   2:9,14,17-18

[14] Hebrews   4:14-16;   5:1-3,7-10

[15] Genesis 2:7; 3:19; Psalm 90:3; 103:14; 104:29; Ecclesiastes 12:7

[16] Matthew 1:23; Isaiah 7:14

[17] Luke 1:35; Matthew 1:18, 20-23

[18] Luke 3:23; Matthew 13:55; John 6:42

[19] Hebrews 1:5; Psalm 2:7

[20] Matthew 2:1-12; Luke 2:8-20

[21] Luke   2:39-40

[22] Luke 2:49

[23] Luke 3:23

[24] Matthew 3:1-6; Isaiah 40:3; Malachi 3:1

[25] Matthew   3:13-17

Him... to stay in Him throughout His earthly ministry.[26] Then God's voice resounded from above: "This is My Son, whom I love; with Him I am well pleased."[27] In fact, He found His Son delightful.[28]

LIKE FATHER, LIKE SON

For centuries people had sought a glimpse of God. They may have detected His presence in a trembling mountain[29] or heard His voice for a brief moment, but it seems hard to really understand a God you cannot see. Then Jesus came to earth. He knew His Father inside out, so He came to show us the Father He knew so well.[30]

Jesus was more than a man after God's own heart. He was more than just the friend of God. He was His very offspring. His unique Son.[31] He reflected in all He said and did the exact nature of God.[32] To see Jesus was to see His Father.[33]

To see Jesus constantly pouring out His life for the sick and injured from morning to night is to see God in a new light.[34] "Everyone is looking for You," Simon reported. Jesus reply was, "let's go to them then. This is why I'm here."[35] The untouchable leper appeals for cleansing and Jesus reaches out, touches him, and heals him.[36] God's heart can be touched. He is willing and desires to touch us, even in our diseased condition. Jesus was easily distracted from teaching, then from a trip to help a dying girl by still another woman

---

[26]Matthew 3:16; John 1:32-34; Luke 4:14; John 3:34

[27]Matthew 3:17; Luke 3:22

[28]Isaiah 42:1

[29]Exodus 19:16-25

[30]John 1:18

[31]John 1:14; 3:16; I John 4:9

[32]Hebrews 1:3

[33]John 14:9-11

[34]Matthew 4:23-25; Mark 1:21-34

[35]Mark 1:35-39

[36]Matthew 8:1-4

in need.[37] Good news! God is never too busy to stop and consider your need. Jesus' eyes instinctively went to the bent and crippled woman in the crowd,[38] the one with the greatest need, the most helpless and hopeless. He had His Father's eyes; eyes of compassion and love.

"I am the Lord, your Holy One, Israel's Creator, your King," God proclaimed.[39] He was holy and without sin, and so was His Son.[40] How then do they view weak and flawed humans, sinners? They see them as those who need help, those who need a friend. Jesus ate with them.[41] He was called the friend of tax collectors and sinners. They dared invite Him to dine and He came.[42] A common sinner from the street risked coming to where He was eating with self-righteous men and she received a great blessing.[43] The outcasts of society crowded around to hear Him and He welcomed them.[44] A condemned adulteress found Him willing to lay down His life for her sinful one. He braved insults and possible stones[45] for a wretched sinner.

This is your God. Looking on the crowds of New York, Moscow, and Calcutta with compassion because they are harassed and helpless.[46] Nothing escapes His sympathetic eyes.[47] Everyone touches His tender heart. You can come to Him for help. He will lift you up, not put you down.[48] "Let us then approach the throne of grace with confidence so that we may receive mercy and find grace

---

[37]Mark   5:21-43
[38]Luke   13:10-12
[39]Isaiah 43:15
[40]I Peter 2:22
[41]Matthew 9:10-13; 11:19
[42]Luke   19:1-10
[43]Luke   7:36-50
[44]Luke   15:1-2
[45]John   8:1-11
[46]Matthew 9:36
[47]Hebrews 4:13
[48]James   1:5

in our time of need."[49] Praise God. He is like Jesus. And Jesus is really something.

MY FATHER AND YOUR FATHER

Jesus had an enviable relationship with His Father. He frequently talked to Him in prayer.[50] Sometimes this lasted all night.[51] He was an obedient Son.[52] Doing His Father's will was His constant desire.[53]

For centuries God had sought intimate relationships with humanity. He was forsaken in the garden by the first couple but He found others, such as Enoch, and Noah's family, Abraham and Sarah; then Isaac, Jacob, and Joseph. "I am the God of Abraham, Isaac and Jacob," He announced to Moses.[54] Not I was, but I am. Always I am.[55] Once God claims you and you claim God, the relationship is forever.[56] Our forever Father seeks forever relationships. Even centuries later God still says, "I am the God of Abraham, Isaac, and Jacob." He is only the God of the living. In Him you never die.[57] So God found Moses, Joshua, Deborah, Gideon, Ruth, Samuel, Hannah, David and a host of others.

From Abraham through the lineage of Jacob He formed a nation upon which to lavish His great affections,[58] but over and over they were an unfaithful people. All He wanted was a people He could

---

[49]Hebrews 4:16
[50]Mark 1:35;Luke 3:21;Matthew 14:23; Luke 5:16; 9:18,28,11:1
[51]Luke 6:12
[52]Hebrews 5:8
[53]John 4:34; 5:30; 6:38; 9:4 Matthew 26:39-42
[54]Exodus 3:6
[55]Notice Exodus 3:14
[56]John 3:16-17; Hebrews 13:5; John 20:31; I John 1:1-2; 5:13
[57]Matthew 22:29-33; John 11:25-26
[58]Deuteronomy 7:1-11

abundantly bless who would love Him and call Him Father,[59] but finally God can only say of these people, "all day long I have held out my hands to a disobedient and obstinate people."[60]

Jesus comes to show the Father as He has never been shown. It is hard to resist the man from Galilee. His words are simple, powerful and compelling. "No one ever spoke the way this man does."[61] Mothers wanted their babies to feel His touch and children eagerly sought His arms.[62] Some are amazed that the Old Testament says so much about caring for the homeless, widows, strangers and the poor while Jesus said little about these, but the fact is, Jesus did not talk about it - He did it. His every waking hour found Him confronted by the weak, the hurting and the outcast. Never once did He turn one away.

God proclaimed Himself the helper of the fatherless and the widow.[63] He tried to create a nation which would carry out His heart's desire and be a witness of His loving nature to the world.[64] At last His own Son is born. He comes and embodies the very nature of His Father. All the righteous demands of the law, and specifically those to care for the poor and needy, were fulfilled in Jesus' life.[65]

No wonder the Father changes Jesus appearance to a dazzling brightness. No wonder He eclipses Moses the great lawgiver and Elijah the great prophet. No wonder the voice of the Father announces "This is My Son, whom I love; with Him I am well pleased. Listen to Him!"[66] He is more than an angelic messenger.

---

[59]Jeremiah   3:19-20
[60]Isaiah 65:2; Romans 10:21
[61]John 7:46; Matthew 7:28-29; 13:54; Luke 4:31-32
[62]Mark 10:13-16; Matthew 19:13-15; Luke 18:15-17
[63]Psalm 68:5-6; 10:14; Deuteronomy 10:18
[64]Deuteronomy 10:19; Leviticus 19:33-34; Isaiah 43:10-13; 44:6-8
[65]Matthew 5:17-18; John 17:4; 19:30
[66]Matthew 17:1-5

Infinitely more.[67] He is greater than Moses and more than a law-giver.[68] He is much more than a prophet for He did not come merely to announce words, but to live the words. He was the Word, the living Word,[69] and His Father placed all authority in His hands. All of it.[70] And Jesus used this power to hold out to you the right to become children of God.[71]

It was like a great conspiracy; a conspiracy of love. Jesus came to show the irresistible character of His Father. When you are drawn to Him, He then turns you over to His Father who cleanses you and keeps you in His love forever. What a Son! What a Father!

To Mary in the morning mist Jesus said, "I am returning to My Father and your Father, to My God and your God."[72] He came to make His Father, your Father. It doesn't get better than this.

THE FATHER AND HIS SUFFERING SON

Much has been said about the great suffering of Jesus Christ on the cross for our sins, and much more should be said, but we should also remember that when Jesus was lied about, spit on, flogged, and finally cruelly executed, His loving Father watched the whole scene.

Then the great moment of moments arrived. Jesus is hanging impaled on the cruel cross. Insensitive fools mock Him from below. The burden of all the sins of the world weighs mightily on Him. He looks upward to His Father, the Father to whom He had prayed hours earlier "if it is possible, may this cup be taken from me".[73]

---

[67]Hebrews 1:4-14

[68]Hebrews 3:1-6

[69]John 1:1-4,14

[70]Matthew 28:18; Daniel 7:13-14; Luke 10:22; John 3:35; 17:2; I Corinthians 15:27-28; Ephesians 1:19-23; Philippians 2:9-11; Acts 2:33; Romans 14:8-12; Colossians 2:9-10

[71]John 1:12-13

[72]John 20:16-18

[73]Matthew 26:39

He looks up to His Father, but He isn't there. "My God, My God, why have you forsaken Me?" He cries in deep anguish.[74]

How could He forsake His beloved Son, the One who always obeyed, the One who was His delight. God had a choice; it was us or Him. And in compassion and love, He incredibly chose us and let His Son die.[75] The perfectly good died for the bad "to bring you to God".[76]

How He wants you to know His Father. "How great is the love the Father has lavished on us, that we should be called children of God."[77]

---

[74]Matthew 27:46
[75]Romans 5:6-8
[76]I Peter 3:18
[77]I John 3:1

1. Why is it important that Jesus be understood as both the son of man and the Son of God?

2. What kind of relationship did Jesus have with the Father? Describe it in some detail.

3. In discovering God's nature, what does Jesus contribute to our search?

4. Try to describe the extent of your Father's caring compassion as revealed in the life of Jesus. How does this compare to your compassion?

5. What had God sought throughout the centuries which was finally realized in the life of His Son, Jesus?

6. Read Hebrews 1. How does Jesus compare to the angels?

7. How does Jesus exceed great men like Moses and Elijah?

8. What is the primary use that Jesus makes of the all-inclusive authority given Him by His Father?

9. What could have possibly compelled the Father to forsake His Son and allow Him to suffer and die on the cross?

10.What is the significance of the phrase from John 20:17 - "My Father and your Father"?

Notes

God's chosen people Israel called Him "God" or "Lord", and this was fine, but what He really longed to be called was "Father".[1] He proclaimed that He cared for them even more than a nurturing mother,[2] but Israel kept Him at a safe distance and never as a people referred to Him as their Father.

One day however, an Israelite named Jesus sat down on a Galilean mountainside and taught for a few minutes.[3] Twice He spoke of God[4] but then called Him "your Father in heaven".[5] Seventeen times He specifically called God "Father" in this brief message.[6] This must have sounded strange to their ears and was probably a bit disturbing.

Jesus was determined to reveal His wonderful Father to mankind, to remove the veil which seemed to prevent His people from clearly knowing and understanding Him,[7] or passionately loving Him. Jesus knew the great heart of His Father for He was His Son, and they were as One.[8] So He told a story, a beautiful story designed to reveal to us the magnitude of His great Father's heart... a story we would never forget.[9]

---

[1] Jeremiah 3:4,19; also see Psalm 89:26; Isaiah 63:16; 64:8
[2] Isaiah 66:13; 49:15-16
[3] Matthew chapters 5-7
[4] Matthew 5:8,9
[5] Matthew 5:16
[6] Matthew 5:16,45,48; 6:1,4,6,8,9,14,15,18,26,32; 7:11,21
[7] II Corinthians 3:13-18
[8] John 10:30; 7:21-23
[9] Luke 15:11-32

THERE WAS A MAN WHO HAD TWO SONS

Jesus attracted unusual crowds. The tax collectors, sinners and outcasts flocked to His feet.[10] Such a crowd had come to hear Jesus teach. The religious leaders murmured on the sidelines, "this man welcomes sinners and eats with them".[11] Jesus did this because He was just like our Heavenly Father. He came to seek and save the lost.[12] The Father and His Son planned to bring us into fellowship with them.[13] It was a most holy conspiracy. So to this divided audience, Jesus told His story.

He told of a father who had two sons. The father here is obviously to be understood as being His Heavenly Father. The younger son wanted out. He requested his portion of the estate, so his father complied with his wishes. Some have criticized the father's actions here. Didn't he know the boy would go off and use all that money foolishly? Why didn't he say "no"?

Here we learn a great truth about our Father. He did not make us to be puppets or robots; we are not automatons. We were created in His image to be free. Free to choose...to love and serve God or to reject God and go our own way.[14] He wanted his son at home with him, but this father knew a son held "against his will is of the same persuasion still". He wanted the son to grow up to love him and do what was right, but it had to be from his heart. He had to learn this himself. Our Father loves us beyond our understanding, yet if we choose to turn from Him and go to our "far country", He will let us go.

So the son gathered everything, along with his share of the estate, and went to a distant place where he could live as he pleased... far from the father's eyes. He rapidly wasted his wealth in wild living. Wild living is any living done outside the Father's direction, and any

---

[10]Luke 15:1; also Luke 5:29

[11]Luke 15:2; see also Matthew 9:11

[12]Luke 19:10

[13]John 14:20, 23; I John 1:3

[14]Joshua 24:15

94

expenditure of this world's goods not submitted to the Father's guidance is wasteful.

AFTER HE HAD SPENT EVERYTHING

"Easy come, easy go." It was great while it lasted; wall to wall fun, plenty of friends, plenty of everything...but the day came when it all ran out. It always does, sooner or later. Either the supply will dry up or the things will lose their appeal. There is no life outside the Father.[15] As I was writing this, the newspaper reported that a 24 year old pro basketball player had committed suicide. He had just purchased a new house and his future was bright, but money and fame are not enough. Why are the rich and famous so often users of cocaine? Or other drugs? Because there is a void in their lives...a God-shaped void.

Soon the boy was in need, severe need. He needed food, not to mention a place to stay and clothing. He went looking for a job but none was to be found. Finally a man said he would hire him to feed his pigs. Imagine a Jewish boy who wouldn't *touch* pork feeding pigs.[16] But he was starving. His shoes were worn out and his tunic was ragged. All his jewelry had long ago been hocked. The ring from his father was the hardest to give up. His thoughts turned to his father, but then his hunger brought him back to the present and he began thinking about giving the pigs' food a try.

WHEN HE CAME TO HIS SENSES

One day he decided this was all very ridiculous. He remembered his father and home. He remembered the hearty meals the farm-hands enjoyed. Here he was in a pigpen hungrily eyeing pigs' food and his father's hired men were chowing down and had food to spare. His father always took good care of everyone. So does our Father.

He decided he would head home He knew his father well enough to know he'd have a good chance of being taken in. After all, dad was a pretty decent guy. So he began to rehearse his speech. He would confess his sinfulness and failure. He would admit his actions had

---

[15]John 14:6
[16]Leviticus 11:7-8

95

disqualified him as a son. His behavior had been shameful and had reproached his father's good name. He would plead with his father to make him like the other hired men. He headed home because life on his own in rebellion to his father had failed...as it always does. It was hard for him to get started, but finally he arose and began trudging homeward.

As he grew closer, fear must have gripped his heart. Could he bear his father's deserved rebuke? What if he told him to get off the place? How would he explain his empty pockets, his filthy, ragged clothes, and the smell of the pigpen? He almost turned back several times, but where would he go? His legs and his resolve must have weakened with each mile. He was still a long way from home. He didn't think he could make it.

BUT WHILE HE WAS STILL A LONG WAY OFF

His brokenhearted father had never given up. He had heard stories of his son's foolish living. He longed to go and drag him home and shake some sense into him, but the father knew this would never work. (Likewise, our Father will leave us in our sinfulness until we are ready to come home.) Yet the word was out: "If anyone sees my wayward son heading this way, please let me know." The message traveled fast, faster than the heavy-footed and defeated son. While he was still at a distance the father heard. It was no mistake. He was thinner and looked frightful, but it was him.

What would the father do? Wait for the boy to crawl home and grovel a bit? Refuse to see him for a while maybe? No! The father dropped what he was doing and headed down the road toward his sin-weary son. Then he saw him far down the road. He knew it was his son. He looked so tired and small. He looked like a whipped puppy. He looked like he was on his last legs. He might never make it all the way home.

The father's heart swelled until it nearly burst. All the hurt and shame and painful waiting -- well, that was yesterday. Tears blurred the father's eyes. His pace increased instinctively. All his great compassion gushed to the surface. Suddenly he could begin to make out his face. It was more than he could stand. He began running. Staid Jewish custom forbade a mature man to run. It was undignified. But this is my son! He's coming home!

96

When Jesus related in this story that the father "ran to his son', He revealed an astounding truth: God loves His sinful children so much, He will run out to meet us if we will come home to Him. Will God run?[17] Yes, in order to come to the aid of His beloved children, even when they smell of the far country.

The startled son saw his father coming. He was running. The son must hurry and deliver his prepared speech. "Father, I have sinned against heaven and against you," he cried. Now his father was ever so near. He saw tears which were collecting in his beard. How good his father's face looked. Quickly he exclaimed, "I am no longer worthy to be called your son!" Two points down and one to go. Too late. His father moved faster than he had expected. Suddenly he was encompassed in a mighty hug. Warm kisses covered his neck and face.

His father never allowed him to finish his speech - the part about making him a hired servant. The father didn't want a servant - he wanted his son. "Bring the robe, the ring and the sandals. Kill the fatted calf and let's have a feast and celebrate. For this son of mine was dead and is alive; he was lost and is found.

The father is God. And He is always like this. Such a Father! How blessed to be His son or daughter!

BUT THE FATHER HAD ANOTHER SON

In from the field came the other son who had stayed home and worked faithfully for the father. What was all this commotion? He was informed that his wayward brother had come home and all this celebrating was for his brother.

His jealousy and anger erupted to the surface. The father came out to encourage him to join the celebration. No way! "This son of yours," he said (not, "my brother"),"goes off and 'has a ball' wasting everything with wild women and then just prances back home and you accept him. You never had any celebrations for me." (Had he ever asked? Would he have enjoyed it?)

---

[17]See Charles Hodge's book, Will God Run?

Somehow this attitude sounds familiar. Suppose a member of the church falls away for a couple of years and isn't heard from. Then one Sunday he somehow musters the courage to come to the assembly, and then he comes the next week and the next. He becomes active again; he has come home.

It is often suggested that he must publicly confess his unfaithfulness and ask the church's forgiveness. He can't just come back and take up his place like nothing happened. However, the only thing that matters is whether the Father has accepted him back. If He has, then dare we the brothers and sisters question his standing with the Father? If one comes home to the Father, we should simply join in the celebration and the joy of the Father. He owes us no explanation - that's between him and the Father.

COMING TO GRIPS WITH OUR FATHER'S LOVE

Our Father's heart is immensely larger than we imagine. We must never try to squeeze God into our undersized view of Him. We must allow our minds and heart to be ever expanded so we can begin to grasp the eternity[18] of His love, as well as its astounding width, depth and height.[19]

Let us think often of the father in Luke 15 for He is our Father. He is always waiting for us. Let us gaze on His beautiful nature so that we may, day by day, be changed into His likeness.[20] O, our Father, please let it happen!

---

[18]Jeremiah 31:3

[19]Ephesians 3:18-19; see also Job 11:7-9

[20]II Corinthians 3:18

1. Why would God not be content to be called "Lord" or "Master" rather than the title "Father"?

2. Why was Jesus always so often involved with outcasts and sinners? How is the church doing in this respect?

3. Why did the Father allow the rebellious son to leave with his goods?

4. What does the Father do about His children who are away indulging themselves in their "far country"?

5. What are some "far countries" which we encounter today?

6. What turned this son around and started him on the road home? Where is home?

7. What is the significance of each of the three parts of the son's speech?

8. How did the Father react when He saw His son coming home?

9. What was wrong with the older brother? How are we like this?

10. What do we learn here about the nature of God?

Notes

13   THE FATHER HE WANTS TO BE TO YOU

You were created to be a child of God. You will never find peace until you settle willingly into that position. As you continue to study about your heavenly Father, and as you deeply meditate upon His nature and character, one truth will arise again and again: "How great is the love the Father has lavished on us, that we should be called children of God! And that is what we are!"[1] No matter what else you are or ever become, above all else you need to accept your role as His child. You were never too young, nor will you ever grow too old, to need the Fatherly care of God.

Sometimes your Father seems so real and near, but too often He seems off in the distance or hidden altogether. Be certain it is not your Father who has drifted away or left for a while. He is your Father "who does not change"[2] and in watching over you, He never slumbers or sleeps.[3] He will never leave you or forsake you.[4] His faithfulness continues for all generations.[5] Our Lord Jesus Christ who is "the radiance of God's glory and the exact representation of His being"[6] is exactly "the same yesterday and today and forever."[7] Count on it!

What happens is, you and I drift away. We foolishly get caught up in other pursuits. "The worries of this life, the deceitfulness of wealth and the desire for other things",[8] Jesus called them, and He was right. And then we fail to "fix our eyes on Jesus".[9] So we start to sputter and and struggle. Like sheep, we begin to go astray. All

---

[1] I John 3:1
[2] James 1:17
[3] Psalm 121:3-4
[4] Hebrews 13:5
[5] Psalm 100:5
[6] Hebrews 1:3
[7] Hebrews 13:8
[8] Mark 4:19
[9] Hebrews 12:2

of us. You too![10] But our Father cannot accept this. His love is too intense. He sees the crowds, harassed and helpless, like sheep without a shepherd.[11] He sees you. And He springs into action.

IN COMPASSION OUR FATHER SEEKS US

Early on, your sensitive Father detects your movement away from Him and He comes looking for you. You may be slinking about in your forest of guilt and shame and frustration, but if you listen, you can hear Him calling, "where are you?"[12] You need only say, "Here I am, Father. I have sinned and acted foolishly" and He will always forgive you and take you back.[13] Always.

However sometimes you feel so unexplainably alone. You feel "without hope and without God in the world".[14] It's like when you were a small child and you got lost from your parents in a strange store. There was no hope -- no way you could find your way out to safety, to home. You were frightened and crying and in near panic, but they found you, didn't they? Why? Because they would not leave until every aisle was scanned, every corner examined. Every possible spot was searched - and suddenly they were there, holding you, and all hope was restored. So it is with your Father.

God's Son is the Chief Shepherd.[15] When you are like a sheep going astray, He goes out looking for you. How long does He search? "Until He finds it."[16] Then He will lift you on His shoulder and tenderly carry you home.[17] He wishes you would grow up and learn to stay home, but He knows your weaknesses and never tires of rescuing and forgiving you. You are His precious jar of clay[18]

---

[10]Isaiah 53:6; Romans 3:9-18

[11]Matthew 9:36

[12]Genesis 3:9

[13]I John 1:8-10

[14]Ephesians 2:12

[15]I Peter 5:4

[16]Luke 15:4

[17]Luke 15:5; I Peter 2:25

[18]Psalm 103:8-14; II Corinthians 4:7

which is being shaped into His image[19] and will someday be endowed with His eternal existence.[20] Unfortunately, the straying from the Father sometimes goes farther...much farther. Have you ever traveled so far from God that His voice no longer can be heard? This is called the "far country", the land away from God.[21] When you go there, what does the Father do?

WAITS AND DRAWS YOU WITH HIS ENDLESS LOVE

Millions in our nation, including many in the church, periodically drift into rather severe depression. You may be one of them. When you are there you feel almost cut off from all that makes life worth living, and there you cannot hear the voice of the Father.[22] The Psalmist David several times praises God for either keeping him out of the pit or for delivering him from the pit and setting him again on joyful ground.[23] I believe David means the pit of despair and depression. He had passed from deep distress to having his heart filled with great joy. Then he was able to "lie down and sleep in peace".[24] But how did our Father deal with those who were in depression?

A period in Elijah's life is most enlightening on the subject.[25] After some great victories[26] Elijah's life was threatened by Queen Jezebel. For some reason the prophet really let this get him down. He became severely depressed, withdrew from his daily life and asked God to let him die. His loving Father did not chide him or tell him to get up and get busy. He fed him (though Elijah didn't want it), let him sleep, and then fed him again. He followed Elijah up Mt. Horeb to his new hiding place. God stayed with him. He always does.

---

[19]II Corinthians 3:18

[20]I Corinthians 15:42-44, 53-54

[21]Luke 15:13

[22]See Psalm 10:1; 13:1-2; 22:1-2. In these passages David appears to be depressed and feeling that God is not near of listening.

[23]Psalm 30:1-3; 40:1-3; 103:4-5

[24]Psalm 4:1,6-8

[25]I Kings 19:1-18

[26]I Kings 18:16-45

After letting Elijah have some time (several weeks), He came to him and gently asked, "what are you doing here, Elijah?" Elijah shot back his complaints. God listened. Then God asked him to stand out on the mountain in His presence because He was going to come to Elijah in a significant way. Still Elijah huddled in his cave of withdrawal. Then God acted. First came a ferocious wind, followed by an earthquake and then a fire, but God was not in any of these. Finally, there came only a gentle whisper. And slowly God restored Elijah to useful life and service. Notice, the Father did not try to blow the depressed Elijah away with strong words, or shake some sense into him, or lash out at him with heated rebukes. Rather, He gently awakened his tired and hopeless heart with a gentle whisper of love. He waited for Elijah to respond, and then restored him.

You have every reason to believe God will do the same for you when you are depressed or in despair. He does not come to condemn you but to save you.[27] He is always near the brokenhearted and knows how to gently save those crushed in spirit.[28]

Unfortunately, we sometimes allow ourselves to become more and more deeply entrenched in sinful activities until we shut ourselves away from God[29] What does our Father do? He allows us to remain in our "far country" but He never stops loving us.[30] Instead, He does something else. Precious memories of Him linger in the heart. He keeps tugging at us. He never lets us go. Because He loves us more than we can imagine, He keeps drawing us toward home.[31]

---

[27]John   3:16-17
[28]Psalm   34:18
[29]Isaiah   59:1-2
[30]Again note Luke 15:11-32
[31]Jeremiah   31:3;   Hosea   11:1-9;   Jeremiah   24:7

ACCEPTS US WARMLY AND WITH FORGIVENESS

The Father loves the heart that is sick of sin, and broken and crushed,[32] because He knows the only steps you have left are steps which lead home... to Him. And when you get home, there is always a lavish welcome and great rejoicing[33] as well as complete forgiveness.[34] As His child, you have a compelling invitation to come directly to the throne of your Father where you always will receive mercy and find grace to help you in your time of need.[35]

Jesus, in His most trying moment, cried out to His Father.[36] He called upon Him using two words for Father. One was Greek; the other, Aramaic. Many scholars suggest that the Aramaic "Abba" actually is a tender endearment which should be translated "daddy". God was to Jesus, and is to you, the ultimate Father, and when you feel small and lonesome and rather helpless, you may just reach out and claim Him as your "daddy". Actually, He encourages you to do so.[37]

A FINAL PORTRAIT OF THE FATHER

I hope these lessons have stirred you deeply. I hope you see your Father much more clearly. May I leave you with one last portrait for your meditation. Isaiah, in trying to awaken sin-bound Israel, announced to them, "Here is your God." Then he gave a brief but poignant picture of the full range of His nature.[38] He says He is the powerful, ruling Sovereign Lord. He is able to reward and repay all who have dwelt on earth. He is awesomely powerful! But look again. He is also a tender shepherd.[39] His strong shepherd arms and hands can be ever so gentle. See Him lift the frightened lamb up and

---

[32]Psalm 51:17; Isaiah 57:15-19

[33]Luke 15:7,22-24

[34]Isaiah 1:18-20; Psalm 32:1-5; Psalm 103:8-14

[35]Hebrews 4:14-16

[36]Mark 14:36

[37]Romans 8:15-17; Galatians 4:6-7

[38]Isaiah 40:9-11

[39]Ezekiel 34:1-31; John 10:1-18

effortlessly carry it as long as is needed. As long as is needed! See Him cuddle it close to His heart until all fear subsides. See how patient and gentle He is with the ewes which are still sore from lambing.

This powerful and compassionate Shepherd is your Father. I close with a poem written by my wife and leave you in the hands of the loving Eternal I AM.[40]

> The eyes of the loving Shepherd
>   roam throughout the land,
> Seeking signs of danger;
>   holding me in his hand.
> Safe, secure and warm am I
>   pressed against His breast,
> The Lion roars, stalking me;
>   peacefully I rest --
> Knowing that my Shepherd,
>   though pierced and wounded sore,
> Guards me,
>   will never leave me,
> Lays His life down at the door.

-Phyllis Phillips-

1988

---

[40]Exodus 3:14

1. What are the basic causes of you or I seeming to be far away from God?

2. When we drift away from God and feel alone and lost, what does He do?

3. Discuss the role of the shepherd when sheep are straying as this relates to our Father/Shepherd and His son the Lord Jesus.

4. Generally, when we go so far away from God in our rebellion and sin that we cannot hear His voice, what does the Father do?

5. Using Elijah's story as an example, how does it appear that our father deals with depression?

6. What do you think was the significance of the wind, earthquake, fire and the whisper in I Kings 19:11-13?

7. Scriptures indicate the Father loves a broken and crushed spirit. Why would a loving Father love such as this?

8. What seems to be the significance for us in the Biblical phrase "Abba, Father"?

9. Is our Father primarily a powerful, sovereign Lord or a gentle, tender Shepherd

10. What are personal thoughts that you have about your Shepherd-Father?

APPENDIX: SUGGESTIONS FOR TEACHERS

Three approaches that can be utilized in teaching this material:

1. Teach the material in 13 weeks using a mixture of lecture and class discussion based on the questions included at the end of each chapter.

2. Teach the material over a 26 week (two quarter) period utilizing two weeks for each lesson.

   Week one: Introduce the lesson utilizing many of the scriptures referenced in the lesson text.

   Week two: After reviewing the previous weeks presentation, use the end of the chapter questions to stimulate discussion.

3. Small group discussion:

   This approach is best suited for groups of 7-12 people with a designated discussion leader who is well prepared.

   Each student should study the week's lesson material beforehand, including the questions at the end of the chapter, and comes to the class primed to share in the discussion.

   The discussion leader facilitates the discussion centering on the significant points in the lesson.

Important Suggestion for Bible Class Teachers:

1. Start your preparation early in the week. These lessons contain vitally and eternally important material. Set aside the necessary time and make the effort to prepare thoroughly to teach. Go at it hard all week. Share with the class the masterpiece you have fashioned. Leave the discarded shavings of preparation behind.

2. After reading through each chapter, go back through and drink deeply from the numerous scripture references provided.

3. As the teacher, you too should carefully write out your own responses to the discussion questions included at the end of each chapter. After you have allowed your class members to share their answers to the questions, you'll be prepared to respond with yours.

4. As you study, take notes of discoveries you make and things which interest and excite you. These likely will excite your class members as well. Write down everything. From these notes, and your memory, you can construct your lesson presentation or structure the class for group discussion.

5. Use this book as a study guide into the scripture. There are over 600 footnotes incorporating over 1000 references to the Bible. Study these many references and you will have an abundance of reliable ideas to draw upon. God's nature is found in the God-breathed scriptures. Plunge in deeply.

6. Start becoming an excited (and exciting) Bible scholar. If you'll do the hard work required to dig through this material and the footnote references, you will gain a solid foundation for discussing God's nature. Out of knowing and understanding God, you will possess the basis for a real relationship with God and for grasping all that God has for you. In other words, let God take you on an absorbing adventure near to His side and you will obtain both great information and a compelling experience to share with your fellow students. Go for it!

Some related books you might enjoy:

God and Man: Then and Now by John T. Willis, professor of Bible at Abilene Christian University. (Also any of his books or tapes on the Old Testament Prophets.)

Knowing God by J.I. Packer

The God You Can Know by Dan DeHaan

Will God Run by Charles Hodge

Your God Is Too Small by J. B. Phillips

If you have any questions or comments, or if you are interested in having Dale conduct a weekend seminar or address your group, you may contact him at:

Dale Phillips
c/o Dryden Publishers
P.O.Box 342
Findlay, OH   45839-0342

DRYDEN PUBLISHERS